DATE			

GREAT NAMES IN BLACK COLLEGE SPORTS

BY DONALD HUNT

MASTERS PRESS

A Division of Howard W. Sams & Company

Published by Masters Press (A Division of Howard W. Sams & Company)
2647 Waterfront Pkwy. E. Dr., Suite 100
Indianapolis, IN 46214

Published 1996

Printed in the United States of America

96 97 98 99 00 01 02   10 9 8 7 6 5 4 3 2 1

Library of Congress Cataloging-in-Publication

Hunt, Donald, 1955-
    Great names in black college sports / by Donald Hunt.
        p. cm.
    ISBN: 1-57028-104-1
    1. Afro-American athletes--Biography. 2. College athletes--United States--Biography. 3. Afro-Ameircan universities and colleges.
I. Title.

GV697.A1H85 1996
796'.092'2--dc20   96-34234
                                                             CIP

ACKNOWLEDGMENTS

Writing this book was something I had envisioned for quite some time in hopes of bringing a greater awareness to black college sports. But I couldn't have accomplished this project without the help of many sports organizations across the country.

First, I would like to thank the publicity departments of the Chicago Bears, San Francisco 49ers, Kansas City Chiefs, Washington Redskins, Houston Oilers, Detroit Lions, Dallas Cowboys, Pro Football Hall of Fame, New York Knicks, New Jersey Nets, Golden State Warriors, Boston Celtics, Basketball Hall of Fame, Atlanta Braves, Florida Marlins, Temple University, Grambling State University, Rutgers, Women's Sports Foundation, Southern Intercollegiate Athletic Conference, Central Intercollegiate Athletic Association, Southwestern Athletic Conference and Mid-Eastern Athletic Conference for sending information and photos of many of the great athletes profiled in this book.

Second, I would like to thank Herm Rogul, former *Bulletin* and *Philadelphia Tribune* sports columnist, for his suggestions and editing of the manuscript. Lastly, I would like to thank my wife, Pat, and son, Little Don, who exhibited a great deal of patience and understanding during the days I was writing and researching information for the book.

CREDITS

Cover Design by Kelli Ternet
Inside photos as credited
Edited by Kim Heusel
Text Layout by Kim Heusel

FOREWORD

While growing up in Philadelphia, I wasn't exposed to many black colleges other than Lincoln University and Cheyney State. But the tradition of the Howards, Gramblings, Tennessee States, Hamptons and Winston-Salems was ever present.

As an adult, I've had the pleasure of being exposed to black college athletics through my position as sports director at Black Entertainment Network. If *you* haven't had the same experience, you don't know what you've missed.

Some historically black college athletic programs date back to the early 1900s and maybe some further back than that, but the excitement of a Saturday football game or a basketball game, whether in a modern dome or a band box of a gym, has not and will not change. Over the past 20 years, I've been in many of those stadiums, both big and small, and in many of those gyms to broadcast black college games, and the memories from those experiences will live forever.

I could write forever about the contests I've witnessed and the athletes who stood out in those games, but the one team that will always stand out in my mind is the Mississippi Valley Delta Devils that featured Willie Totten at quarterback and Jerry Rice at wide receiver. I called this team the greatest show on earth. Week in and week out, game in and game out, when these two athletes put on their uniforms the fans were guaranteed to get a show, not only on the field but along the sidelines with the man who put this great tandem together — coach Archie "The Gunslinger" Cooley.

I truly believe that Archie Cooley was ahead of his time. He had the run-and-shoot before it became popular, he had the no-huddle, he had all the things you see in the other colleges and the pros are using now, and of course, he had Totten and Rice in what was known around the nation as the "Satellite Express."

There are a number of games that stand out in my mind when I think of that team like the matchup with Alcorn State in Jackson, Miss., a game that produced the largest crowd in Mississippi Veterans Memorial Stadium history as well as a classic matchup between Isaac Holt, the All-American defensive back from Alcorn State and Rice. If memory serves me correctly, Holt had a pretty decent game against Rice, holding him to about 11 catches. That was a good day for anybody against Rice.

But that's not the game I want to talk about. The one I remember most occurred in Mumford Stadium on the campus of Southern University in Baton Rouge, La. It was the fourth game of the 1984 season for the Southern Jaguars who were 3-0 going into the critical matchup with Mississippi Valley. Not only was the stadium packed but I was broadcasting to a national TV audience.

Southern had some big guns in quarterback Herman Coleman, running back James Evans and wide receiver Connell Swain, and at half-time led Mississippi Valley by two touchdowns.

The old saying, "It's not over until it's over," was never more true than it was that day. Mississippi Valley came out in the second half and cut through the Southern defense like a hot knife in butter. The Delta Devils scored every time they had the ball and not one scoring drive lasted more than a minute. Once they had the ball they would be in the end zone three or four plays later, and ended up winning the game 63-45.

Mississippi Valley finished the season with a 9-2 record behind the play of Totten and Rice, but those two didn't do it alone. Leading the way was an offensive line that averaged 300 pounds. Not surprisingly, they were called the "tons of fun."

They also had a running back in Carl Byrum who gained more than 1,000 yards, but those figures were overshadowed by Totten's 5,000 yards plus passing and 58 touchdown passes, 28 of them to Rice. Rice caught 100 passes in his junior season and another 112 his senior year.

A lot of programs have tried to duplicate the 1984-85 Mississippi Valley football team. Some may have come close, but in my mind, the Delta Devils of that year remain the greatest show I've ever witnessed in black college football.

Rice's story is just one of many that will follow in *Great Names in Black College Sports*. I know without a doubt that you are going to enjoy it.

Charlie Neal
Sports Director, Black Entertainment Network

TABLE OF CONTENTS

Introduction

Only a handful of the country's top black high school athletes select black colleges. They usually favor athletic powers such as UCLA, Penn State or Notre Dame. That's fine, because those universities not only can provide a good education, but also national television exposure and an appearance in a major football bowl or a trip to the Final Four.

The problem is, some of these black athletes will be lost in the shuffle of major college sports, a world in which failure to make an immediate contribution often means a career on the bench. This does not happen at black colleges.

For many years, black colleges had a stranglehold on the nation's finest black athletes. But when predominantly white universities such as Alabama, Tennessee and Florida started recruiting blacks in the mid-70s, the black schools were stripped of the best talent.

Despite the present situation, black colleges have been just as prolific as white colleges in producing professional athletes over the last 15 years. Some of the best players in professional sports are from black colleges: Jerry Rice (Mississippi Valley State, San Francisco 49ers), Charles Oakley (Virginia Union, New York Knicks), Marquis Grissom (Florida A&M, Atlanta Braves).

Locally, the track and field program at Lincoln University, my alma mater, has won several NCAA championships under head coach Cyrus Jones. Ron (Fang) Mitchell, the head basketball coach of Coppin State, guided the Eagles to the Mid-Eastern Athletic Conference's first postseason basketball victory in years by defeating St. Joseph's in the 1995 NIT.

The black colleges may no longer be getting the top athletes, but they continue to develop these athletes to their full potential — without a lot of money or television exposure. Even more important, black colleges have produced some of the country's finest educators, business people, entertainers, journalists and politicians, people such as Thurgood Marshall (Supreme Court justice, Lincoln), Spike Lee (actor and director, Morehouse), Debbie Allen (actress,

Howard University), Ed Bradley (CBS newsman, Cheyney) and many others.

Right now, there is a perception among black athletes that they have to go to a major Division I school in order to be successful. These athletes should be told by coaches, teachers and guidance counselors that is not the case. Not everyone has the ability to compete in major-college sports. But most athletes can play for a black college as well as get an outstanding education.

Great Names
in Black College
Sports

Anthony Mason

Ask Anthony Mason what former Tennessee State star played for the New York Knicks 1969 NBA championship team, he'll give the answer immediately.

"That's easy man," Mason said. "It's Dick Barnett. Everybody who has followed the Knicks over the years knows about Dick Barnett.

"He was before my time, but people used to tell me about his left-handed jump shot where he kicked his feet back," Mason continued. "He used to hit nothing but the net in the (Madison Square) Garden. I'm sure he killed them with that shot during his days at Tennessee State."

Before a summer 1996 trade to the Charlotte Hornets, Mason was the Knicks' third player from Tennessee State behind Leonard (Truck) Robinson, who won an NBA rebounding championship. The 6-foot-7-inch, 250-pound forward finished fifth on Tennessee State's all-time scoring list with 2,075 points. In 1987-88, Mason averaged a career-high 28 points a game to lead the Ohio Valley Conference.

©George Kalinsky

Anthony Mason

"I had a pretty good college career," Mason said. "I really enjoyed playing for Tennessee State. They have a good basketball tradition. The school has produced some fine players like Truck Robinson, Lloyd Neal and most recently Carlos Rogers who plays for the Toronto Raptors. I just wished I could have gone a little higher in the draft. Maybe things would have been a little easier for me."

In 1988, Mason, a native of Queens, New York, where he received All-City honors at Springfield Gardens High School, was drafted by Portland in the third round. He went on to play professionally in Turkey for a few months.

After his draft rights were relinquished by the Trail Blazers, he later signed with New Jersey as a free agent in 1989, but missed the first half of the season with a stress fracture in his right foot.

In 1990, Mason averaged 29.9 points and 14.8 rebounds for the Continental Basketball Association's Tulsa Fastbreakers. That same year, he signed a 10-day contract with the Denver Nuggets and played three games averaging 3.3 points.

Mason continued to work on his game in the summer of 1991. He averaged 27.8 points for the Long Island Surf and led the United States Basketball League with 11.2 rebounds.

He signed with New York as a free agent in 1991 and developed into a key player for the Knicks, averaging seven points and seven rebounds a game as the team's sixth man. A slim, stylish shooter and ball handler in college, Mason has bulked up and now is capable of playing the game with finesse and power. He just needed an opportunity to play the game.

Over the next five years, Mason played a huge role in the Knicks' playoff success, including their 1994 trip to the NBA finals. In 1995, he was named the NBA's Sixth Man of the Year, chosen over Charlotte's Dell Curry and San Antonio's Chuck Person.

Anthony Mason, a former standout at Tennessee State, played an important role in the New York Knicks' success. (New York Knicks photo, © George Kalinsky)

Mason was the first Knick to receive a major postseason award since Mark Jackson earned Rookie of the Year honors in 1987. He averaged 9.9 points and 8.4 rebounds a game. Mason's ability to handle the ball in the open court, shoot from the perimeter and power the ball inside makes him one of the league's most versatile players.

Mason also has very active life in the community. He's a regular participant in the Maurice Stokes Memorial Charity Game at Kutsher's Country Club and also spends time addressing community groups and athletic teams in his hometown.

CHARLES OAKLEY

When you think about big men who have dominated the Central Intercollegiate Athletic Association, one of the first names that comes to mind is Charles Oakley.

A 6-foot-9-inch, 240-pound forward, Oakley played for head coach David "White Shadow" Robbins at Virginia Union where he is the all-time leading rebounder (1,642) and second on the all-time scoring list (2,379). He averaged 24 points and 17.3 rebounds while leading the Panthers to the 1985 CIAA championship and an overall 31-1 record. As a senior that year, Oakley was the NCAA Division II Player of the Year.

Oakley believes playing in the CIAA tournament was one of the highlights of his college career.

"Everybody in New York talks about the Big East Conference Tournament in Madison Square Garden," Oakley said. "These people think the Big East is really something. Well, I can remember playing in front of sold-out crowds every night in the CIAA Tournament. I mean, the Norfolk Scope was sold out for five consecutive nights.

"We had some great ballgames, too. My senior year we beat Norfolk State for the CIAA championship and that game went down to the last shot. The tournament is the best in the country. It just doesn't receive a lot of publicity."

If you think NBA players have a difficult time getting rebounds when he's in the game, then you should have seen the players from Hampton University, Virginia State and Winston-Salem bounce off him. Oakley's strength, power, hustle and shooting touch made him one of the few Division II players chosen in the first round of the NBA draft.

His hometown Cleveland Cavaliers made him their first pick in 1985, but immediately traded him to the Chicago Bulls, where he had an outstanding season and was named to the NBA's All-Rookie Team after averaging 8.9 rebounds a game.

In a brilliant second season with the Bulls, Oakley finished with an NBA-leading 1,074 re-

©George Kalinsky
Charles Oakley

bounds. He was second in the NBA to Charles Barkley with a 13.1 rebounding average, and his 775 defensive rebounds set a Bulls record that still stands.

In 1988, he led the NBA in total rebounds for the second consecutive year with 1,066. However, Oakley was traded from Chicago to New York for center Bill Cartwright and an exchange of first- and third-round draft selections.

Oakley, who had played with Michael Jordan for three years, teamed with Patrick Ewing in New York to form one of the league's strongest frontcourts. In his first season there he averaged 10.5 rebounds a game. Oakley's rough and tough style of play became the signature mark of the Knicks, especially during the Pat Riley era.

Oakley and former Tennessee State star Anthony Mason play a very physical brand of basketball. There's nothing fancy about Oakley's game. Offensively, he pounds the backboards and takes the ball strong to the basket. On defense, he's not afraid to play the other team's

Charles Oakley (right) played for Virginia Union and was a first-round draft choice by the Cleveland Cavaliers. He is now an important part of the New York Knicks.(Photo © George Kalinsky)

top scoring forward or bang with the strongest big men.

Oakley has helped New York to reach the playoffs each of his eight seasons. In 1994, his contributions to the Knicks' drive to the Eastern Conference championship earned him overdue selections to the NBA All-Star Game and the NBA All-Defensive Team.

Oakley, who grew up in Cleveland and attended John Jay High School, was not highly recruited by Division I schools. He appreciates the education that he was able to get at Virginia Union and the opportunity to get to the NBA. Oakley hasn't forgotten the role his alma mater played in his success and annually donates to a scholarship fund at the school.

NATE NEWTON

Nate Newton had an outstanding career as an offensive and defensive lineman for the Florida A&M Rattlers. His blocking exploits earned him All-Mid-Eastern Athletic Conference honors. Newton could clog up the middle of the line but is much better at opening the holes, and was one of the best linemen in black college football in 1982.

Newton said the place to be on Saturday afternoons was the football stadium.

"There's nothing that compares to playing for a black college," he said. "At FAMU, every Saturday afternoon was an event. We played in front of some huge crowds. You had the fraternities and sororities rocking in the stands. You had the bands playing your favorite music. And on the field, you had some of the most exciting football in the country."

Newton had participated in football, basketball, wrestling, and track and field at Jones High School in Orlando, Fla. He said he didn't have a difficult time making up his mind despite opportunities to attend several other colleges.

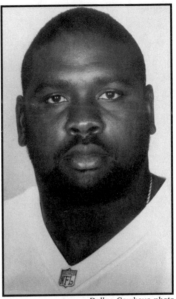

Dallas Cowboys photo
Nate Newton

"I could have gone to a number of colleges," he said. "But I definitely wanted to attend a historically black institution. That's one of the reasons I chose Florida A&M. I wouldn't trade the black college experience for anything in the world. There's nothing like it. All you have to do is go to a black college football game in the fall and you know what I'm talking about."

Despite his successful college career, Newton wasn't drafted by an NFL team. One reason may have been his size. Although he now stands 6 feet, 3 inches tall and weighs in at least 320 pounds, he was a "paltry 275" in college.

"I didn't get real big until I got to the NFL," he said. "I'm a big man now."

Nate Newton (61) never gave up on his dream to play professional football. The former Florida A&M player is now a lineman for the Dallas Cowboys and a three-time Pro Bowler. (Photo courtesy Dallas Cowboys)

But getting to the NFL was not easy. When he wasn't drafted out of college, he signed as a free agent with the Washington Redskins who released him on the final cut of the 1983 summer training camp.

That didn't deter Newton from the pursuit of his desire to play professional football, however. He signed on with the Tampa Bay Bandits in the United States Football League and then hooked up with the Dallas Cowboys just in time to suffer through two of the worst years in Dallas franchise history (1988, 3-13; 1989, 1-15).

Still determined, however, Newton's hard work started to pay off. He became a starting offensive lineman for the Cowboys, who continued to get better and better, and Newton now has three Super Bowl championship rings to show for his dedication.

Possessing outstanding strength and quickness for a man his size, Newton has been one of the Cowboys' most durable players, and a member of three NFC Pro Bowl teams. As a left guard and right tackle, he has started more regular-season games on the offensive line (135) than any other current Cowboy offensive lineman.

Newton and former Central State star Erik Williams have done an excellent job of opening holes for Emmitt Smith, who has been the NFL's top rusher over the last three years.

Many black college players have had to start their careers as free agents. The key to Nate's success was hard work and dedication to his goals. He had to prove he was better than a lot of players from the high-profile college football programs. When given the opportunity, he made the most of it.

"I look around the NFL and see so many black college football players in the league," he said. "I mean, right here in Dallas, Erik (Williams) and I both played for black schools. I'm a big supporter of the black college experience."

He goes back to his college days and credits his coach, Rudy Hubbard, for much of his success and development of his work habits.

"Coach Hubbard gave me an opportunity to develop my game," Newton said. "He refined my skills and just made me a better all-around player. During the time I was there, he was one of the best coaches in the MEAC."

ERIK WILLIAMS

Erik Williams was very disappointed when he couldn't play major college football coming out of Philadelphia's John Bartram High School. "Big E" was recruited by several Division I schools but barely missed the academic requirements to play at those colleges.

Was that the end of the world for him? Not at all. Williams decided to attend Central State in Wilberforce, Ohio, and play for head coach Billy Joe, who is now coach at Florida A&M. The 6-foot-6-inch, 322-pounder, was a small-college All-American for the Marauders, and paved the way for a Central State offense that led the National Association for Intercollegiate Athletics with 492 yards per game and in scoring with a 54.8 average in 1990.

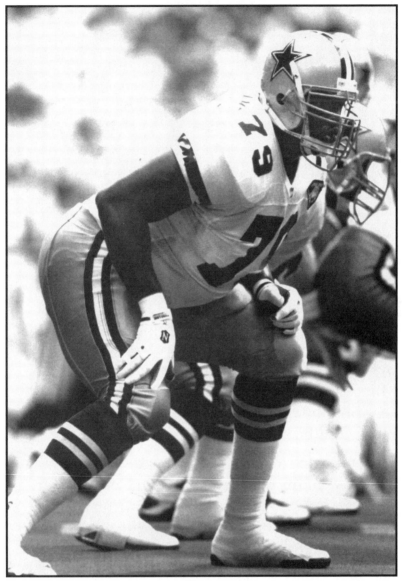

After earning small-college All-American recognition at Central State, Erik Williams has become a Pro Bowl lineman for the Super Bowl champion Dallas Cowboys. (Photo courtesy Dallas Cowboys)

"I originally wanted to play for a major college, but going to Central State may have been the best thing for me," Williams said. "I think getting away from home (Philadelphia) allowed me to grow up."

The Marauders captured the NAIA national title that year with an average winning margin of 33.5 points. In each of Williams' four seasons at Central State, the Marauders never failed to advance to the NAIA playoffs.

Recruited as a defensive tackle, Williams was moved to the offensive line before his freshman season.

"We had some great teams at Central State. We won a lot of football games," Williams said. "Furthermore, I was ready to play in the NFL at the end of my college career."

He gives much of the credit for the success he now enjoys to his college coach, Billy Joe.

"I had an opportunity to play for Billy Joe , who did a good job of working with me," said Williams. "Coach Joe told me I had all the talent to play in the NFL. He told me that my sophomore year."

Although it may have been his dream to play professional football, Williams said he had doubts that he was really that good.

"But coach Joe kept encouraging me every day, and I continued to work on my game," Williams said. "I would have to say he played a key role in my success. I owe a lot to him.

"He was a great disciplinarian. He wanted everybody to work extremely hard, but coach Joe was also fair"

The results of Joe's demands speak for themselves in Central State's record during the time Williams

Dallas Cowboys photo

Erik Williams

played there. And Williams' hard work paid off in 1991 when the Dallas Cowboys made him the first Central State lineman ever drafted by the NFL and only the third player in the history of the school to be selected by the league. The Cowboys picked him in the third round.

Williams started just two games in his first year, but in 1992 he became the starting right tackle and the Cowboys moved Nate Newton to left guard. Williams took full advantage of his opportunity, outplaying Washington defensive end Charles Mann and then Philadelphia defensive end Reggie White.

A year later, Williams played a major role in clearing the way for Emmitt Smith's third straight rushing title and was rewarded with a place on the NFC Pro Bowl team.

As a four-year starter, Williams has developed into one of the top young offensive linemen in the NFL. In 1994, Williams' size, strength and speed enabled him to continue his superb play as the Cowboys got off to a 6-1 start. In the early morning of October 24, however, his season was cut short when he was involved in a car accident, which caused a torn medial collateral ligament, posterior cruciate ligament and popliteal muscle in his right knee.

The subsequent surgery forced him to miss the final half of the season, but Williams was able to make it back in 1995. He is regarded by many pro football experts as the cornerstone of one of the biggest offensive lines in NFL history (averaging 314 pounds per man).

It's hard to believe five offensive tackles were taken before Williams in the draft. But for a kid who grew up a Philadelphia Eagles fan, he's been a huge part of the Cowboys winning three Super Bowls in five years.

As a Philadelphia native, Williams wanted the Eagles to draft him. Instead the Eagles traded up to draft Antone Davis that year. It turned out to be their loss. Williams now enjoys coming home to play against Philadelphia at Veterans Stadium. In addition, Williams and his family distribute great amounts of food and gifts to needy families in West Philadelphia for Thanksgiving.

But he never forgets his days as a student at Central State, and despite his initial disappointment at not being able to play at a larger school, Williams doesn't hesitate in recommending the experience he had for others planning for a college education.

"I think most young people should get a taste of the black college experience," he said. "The history alone is remarkable, especially when you look at the people who have attended so many of these schools. Central State was a good situation for me."

JOHN TAYLOR

When John Taylor showed up on the Delaware State campus as a walk-on, little did anyone know how great a player he was going to be for the Hornets.

A 6-foot-1-inch, 185-pounder, from Pennsauken, N.J., High School, Taylor did not have a brilliant scholastic career. Actually, his best sport was baseball, and he attended Johnson C. Smith College on a baseball scholarship for a year before transferring to Delaware State as a non-scholarship player.

Taylor, a brilliant wide receiver, was named to All-Mid-Eastern Athletic Conference teams from 1983 to 1985. His career totals include 100 receptions for 2,426 yards and 33 touchdowns, four rushing touchdowns, 339 rushing yards and four punts returned for touchdowns.

John Taylor, a standout at Delaware State, made his mark in the NFL with the San Francisco 49ers. (Photo courtesy San Francisco 49ers, © Michael Zagaris)

He established career highs with 40 receptions, 922 yards and 13 touchdowns, while averaging 23.1 yards per catch in 1985, when he was named Player of the Year in the MEAC.

Bill Collick, Delaware State head coach, knows that players like John Taylor don't come around too often.

© *Michael Zagaris*

John Taylor

"He didn't get a lot of publicity," Collick said, "but John Taylor could play the game. He did everything on the field. And he did it all very quietly."

Taylor was a very quiet player and rarely granted interviews with the press. After every game, he usually headed for the showers. It's not that Taylor had anything to hide. He just didn't want to draw a lot of media attention to himself.

"I would rather someone else get the recognition," Taylor said on many occasions. "I just want to go out and play my game."

That's exactly what he did for the Hornets and the San Francisco 49ers. Taylor, a third-round pick in 1986, recently completed a terrific 10-year career with the 49ers.

Taylor teamed up with Jerry Rice to form one of the greatest receiving duos in NFL history. He was on the receiving end of numerous touchdown passes from San Francisco 49ers quarterbacks Joe Montana and Steve Young, and ranks No. 5 among 49er receivers in receptions with 347, No. 4 in receiving yards with 5,598 and No. 2 in yards-per-catch with a 16.1 average.

Taylor holds the club record for the longest scoring play from scrimmage with a 97-yard reception at Atlanta in 1991 and the NFL record of being the only player to score two touchdowns of 90 or more yards in a single game with his scores from 92 and 95 yards against the Los Angeles Rams in 1989.

Taylor has accounted for three of the 49ers' five longest plays. He is the Super Bowl record holder with 94 career punt return yards, and a 15.7-yard average.

Taylor was named by the Pro Football Hall of Fame as a second-team punt return specialist for the NFL's Team of the 1980s and was named as the punt returner for the Silver Anniversary Super Bowl Team by the fans.

As a member of three Super Bowl championship teams, his most memorable championship performance came against the Cincinnati

Bengals in Super Bowl XXIII where he set a Super Bowl record with a 45-yard punt return and caught a game-winning 10-yard touchdown pass from Montana with 34 seconds left.

"John was a player who improved his game each year," said Bill Walsh, former San Francisco 49ers head coach. "He could do a lot of things on the field, and was a great pick for us.

"John made some exciting plays for our ballclub. He was one of the most explosive players on our team. He and Jerry (Rice) formed one of the best receiving tandems in NFL history."

JERRY RICE

If pro football fans think Jerry Rice is unstoppable as an All-Pro wide receiver for the San Francisco 49ers, they should have seen him as a college player at Mississippi Valley State. Playing in a wide-open style offense under coach Archie "The Gunslinger" Cooley, Rice and quarterback Willie "Satellite" Totten, who is now an assistant coach with the Delta Devils, attracted national attention for their offensive exploits.

Rice totaled 4,693 yards and set NCAA Division I-AA records during his four years, and was a consensus All-American with more than 100 receptions in both his junior and senior seasons. As a senior in 1984, he recorded 1,845 yards and scored 28 touchdowns. He exceeded 1,000 yards receiving for three consecutive years,

Jerry Rice, superstar receiver for the San Francisco 49ers, excelled as a student at Mississippi Valley State. (Photo courtesy of San Francisco 49ers, © Michael Zagaris)

using his great moves to elude double coverage. He also displayed a great deal of versatility.

© Michael Zagaris

Jerry Rice

"When you play for a small school, you have to do a lot of different things," Rice said. "I was always learning at Mississippi Valley. Coach Cooley did a great job of letting me develop my skills as an all-around football player.

"Before I went to the NFL, I wanted to be able to run, block and catch. I was fortunate to be in an offense with a good quarterback like Willie (Totten). He knew how to get me the ball in the open field."

Rice was named Most Valuable Player in the Blue-Grey Game, and played in the Freedom All-Star Game. The Crawford, Miss., native was named to the Sheridan Broadcasting Network's Black College Football All-Time Team.

Bill Walsh traded up and drafted Rice in the first round in 1985. He was the third receiver taken, behind Al Toon (10th, New York Jets) and Eddie Brown (13th, Cincinnati Bengals). He set a 49ers rookie record with 927 receiving yards, finishing second on the team to running back Roger Craig (1,014).

"Jerry Rice was a special player," Walsh said. "We saw highlights of him at Mississippi Valley and knew that he would fit in well with Joe Montana. All you have to do with Jerry is just get him the ball. He can do the rest."

During his 11 years in the NFL, Rice has secured a spot in the Pro Football Hall of Fame. He owns NFL career records with 155 touchdowns, breaking Jim Brown's mark of 126 during the 1994 season. His 146 receiving TDs are also the best in NFL history.

A year ago, Rice set a new NFL record of 14,040 receiving yards. He surpassed James Lofton's yardage total of 14,004 receiving yards while eliminating Art Monk as the all-time reception leader with 942 catches.

Rice, 33, is arguably the best receiver to ever play the game. He has made 10 consecutive appearances as a Pro Bowl starter and has 10 consecutive 1,000-yard receiving seasons.

Rice has established Super Bowl career records with 28 receptions, 512 yards, seven touchdowns (and seven receiving TDs) as well as twice setting the Super Bowl single game record with three scores.

CLARENCE

"BIG HOUSE" GAINES

Clarence "Big House" Gaines coached basketball a record 47 years at Winston-Salem State University before retiring in 1993 with 828 victories. His victory total is second only to legendary Kentucky coach Adolph Rupp.

During his coaching career, Big House stood 6 feet, 5 inches tall and weighed more than 250 pounds. When Gaines opened his mouth to speak everybody listened. He had the respect of not only his players, but rival coaches, too.

Gaines posted an amazing 828-447 record at Winston-Salem. In the process, he won 20 or more games 18 times en route to 12 Central Intercollegiate Athletic Association (CIAA) titles.

Probably his most famous player was Earl Monroe. Monroe played on Gaines' 1967 team

Photo courtesy Naismith Basketball Hall of Fame

Clarence "Big House" Gaines

which compiled a 31-1 mark and was the first black college to win an NCAA basketball championship, the NCAA College Division title. That season Gaines was selected as the NCAA College Division Coach of the Year.

"Earl Monroe had a terrific career at Winston-Salem. He did everything on the court," Gaines said. "Then, he went to the NBA and played extremely well for the (Baltimore) Bullets and the (New York) Knicks. Anybody who's seen Earl play knows he can put on a show."

Monroe said he learned a lot from his college coach.

"I was very fortunate to play for one of the legends in basketball — 'Big House' Gaines," Monroe said. "He's one of the greatest coaches of all time. We had a lot of success at Winston-Salem, mostly because of him."

Gaines said Monroe was one of the easiest players to coach.

"He always worked hard in practice," Gaines said of Monroe. "He never had a bad practice. As a matter of fact, he rarely had a bad game. He came to play every day and he got better every year."

In 1978, he was honored with the NABC/MIBA/NIT award; in 1989 he was elected president of the NABC. In 1981, he was elected to the Basketball Hall of Fame in Springfield, Mass.

"No one should be amazed at what coach Gaines has accomplished in his coaching career," said Stephen Smith, college basketball writer for the *Philadelphia Inquirer*. "The man was an outstanding coach. He really paved the way for other black coaches."

One of them is Monte Ross, an assistant coach at St. Joseph's.

"Coach Gaines is one of the kindest individuals I've ever known," said Ross, who played for Gaines at Winston-Salem from 1988-92. "I learned so much from him not only as a player, but as a person, too. He was like a father figure to so many players."

Ross noted that Gaines recruited many players from the Philadelphia area such as Monroe and Teddy Blunt, as well as Leon Whitley and George Gibson. Some other players who went on to basketball fame got away from the great Winston-Salem coach, however.

"Philadelphia is a real hotbed for basketball," Gaines said. "I went to Morgan State (a black college) in Baltimore, Md. Every year I used to go to the Penn Relays, so I knew all about Philadelphia."

He recruited John Chaney, Wilt Chamberlain and Ray "Chink" Scott, but couldn't persuade them to come to Winston-Salem. "I just couldn't get them," Gaines said.

"He used to talk about Earl (Monroe) a lot," Smith recalled. "After every practice he had a story to tell. I feel very fortunate to have had the opportunity to play for him."

Smith also played for Gaines from 1988-91. "I have a real good relationship with him," Smith said. "I try to go down to Winston-Salem to see him two or three times a year. He's really helped me out with contacts in my job as a sportswriter."

Gaines is a great public speaker and educator. "In fact, he didn't have time for guys who just wanted to be basketball players," Smith said. "He wanted them to be more than that. He was always on me about my grades, but he knew I was going to class, and he knew that I wanted to be more than a basketball player."

"I really enjoyed working with the young people," Gaines said. "I had a great time of not only coaching them, but developing players into their full potential on and off the court."

He says the job of coaching at black colleges today is much more difficult than it was when he began coaching.

"Black college coaches have a very tough job," he said. "They aren't getting the same quality of kids today that they did years ago. Consequently, there's a lot more teaching and developing involved to shape the student-athletes. But in spite of the situation, black college coaches are still able to produce some great people."

Gaines took over the head coaching job with the Rams in 1946 but never expected that he could continue to coach for almost a half century. Nevertheless, he was able to influence the lives of many young athletes. His son, Clarence Gaines Jr., is a scout for the Chicago Bulls.

"Coaches come and go, records come and go," Gaines said, "but if you touch peoples' lives, they'll remember you. Winston-Salem gave me a chance to touch a lot of people. I feel I had a chance to make a difference in their lives and that was very important to me."

SAM JONES

Sam Jones, former Boston Celtics standout, was known for his bank shots. A 6-foot-4-inch guard, who could run the floor, hit the boards and score from anywhere on the court, Jones teamed up with Bill Russell, K.C. Jones, John Havlicek, Bob Cousy, Bill Sharman, Tom Heinsohn and Tom Sanders to lead Boston to 10 NBA championships, including eight consecutive titles (1958-66).

As a student at North Carolina College (now North Carolina Central University) Jones scored 1,770 points under Hall of Fame coach John McLendon. Red Auerbach still chose him in the first round of the 1957 NBA draft, on the recommendation of Horace (Bones) McKinney, coach of Wake Forest.

Sam Jones takes the ball to the basket during his professional playing days with the Boston Celtics. (Photo © Dick Raphael)

During an NBA career that spanned 12 years, Jones made five All-Star Game appearances and played in 871 regular-season games and 154 playoff games. He scored 15,411 points (17.7 average) during regular-season play and 2,909 (18.9) in the playoffs.

"The big thing about Sam is that he keeps shooting just the way Bill Sharman used to do," said Red Auerbach, former coach and general manager of the Boston Celtics. "Sam knows he's a good shooter and if he hits a cold spell, he knows it will end sooner or later.

"The difference between Sam and guys like that is that he (Sam) has the guts to throw the ball up there. He knows his job is to score and he isn't afraid to work at it. That's why he was such a clutch player for us over the years."

Jones, who was elected to the Basketball Hall of Fame in 1988, led the Celtics in scoring in three seasons, averaging a career-high 25.9 points per game in 1965.

"One of the great plays in the league is when Sam fakes one way, goes the other and makes someone play him one-one-one," Auerbach added. "There's none who can move like Jones."

Jones admits that he was never shy about taking a shot when he had one. At the same time, he never made a production of his scoring feats, taking them in stride along with his misses.

"I have my good shots and when they come up, I take them," he said. "Sometimes they go in and sometimes they don't, but as long as they are good shots for me, I take them."

A press release put out by the Boston Celtics described Jones this way:

©*Boston Celtics*

Sam Jones

"Of all the great shooters who have worn the Green — Bob Cousy, Frank Ramsey, Bill Sharman, Tommy Heinsohn, to name a few — none had the variety that Sam possessed. He had the suspension shot, jump shot, drive shot, two-handed overhead shot and moves that mystified the best in the game."

In addition to his shooting, Jones exhibited great speed, court vision and savvy.

"Sam Jones has two speeds — fast and real fast," said teammate Bill Russell.

The Celtics press release claims Jones was faster than either of the other two backcourt stars of his day — Jerry West and Oscar Robertson — and his shooting compared favorably with both.

In 1970, Jones was selected to the NBA Silver Anniversary Team, a squad composed of the NBA's brightest stars over the league's first 25 years.

WILLIS REED

Grambling State University has a long tradition of producing great football players, but Willis Reed is the greatest basketball player to ever play for Grambling.

Reed, a 6-foot-10-inch, 240-pound center, led the Tigers to three NAIA tournaments and the 1961 championship. He was taken in the second round of the NBA draft by the New York Knicks and was the NBA's Rookie of the Year after averaging 19.5 points and 14.7 rebounds.

Reed was a left-handed power player with a brilliant outside shooting touch. In 1970 he became the only player to capture MVP honors in the NBA All-Star Game, regular season and playoffs in the same season.

Willis Reed, the greatest basketball player to come out of Grambling University, led the New York Knicks to NBA titles in 1970 and 1973. He later coached the Knicks and then Creighton University before returning to the NBA to coach the New Jersey Nets before becoming the Nets' executive vice president and general manager. (Photo courtesy Basketball Hall of Fame)

He is often remembered for his gutsy performance in the championship series that season against the Los Angeles Lakers. His classic moment came when he hobbled through the tunnel of Madison Square Garden and onto the floor for Game 7.

Reed had injured his knee in Game 5 and it looked as if New York was going to lose the series. But that didn't happen. He made two early baskets and played 27 quality minutes to sparks the Knicks in the Game 7 victory.

"Willis' presence was always a psychological lift for us," said Walt Frazier, the Knicks' point guard.

Reed's hard work and determination enabled the Knicks to win an NBA title not only in 1970, but also in 1973. In 1974, a torn cartilage in his right knee ended his pro career.

Reed, who was elected to the Basketball Hall of Fame in 1981, played with fellow Hall of Famers Dave DeBusschere, Bill Bradley, Walt Frazier, Earl Monroe and Jerry Lucas. "No. 19" was a five-time All-NBA selection and scored 12,183 points (18.7 per game) and grabbed 8,414 rebounds (12.4) during his 10-year career.

Reed's coaching career started in 1977 when he guided the New York Knicks to a 43-39 record and a playoff spot. He spent one season as an assistant coach to Lou Carnesecca at St. John's before taking the head coaching job at Creighton University, where he won a national recruiting war for Benoit Benjamin.

In 1985, Reed returned to the NBA as an assistant with the Atlanta Hawks and made his way through Sacramento before coming to the New Jersey Nets as head coach. He is currently entering his seventh season as executive vice president and general manager of the Nets.

He hired Alfred (Butch) Beard as head coach, making him the first NBA mentor to come directly from a black college (Howard University).

Earl Monroe, who played for Winston-Salem, dazzled foes and thrilled the crowds in college and in the NBA. (Photo courtesy New York Knicks)

EARL MONROE

When Earl Monroe played for Philadelphia's
John Bartram High School, he was a 6-foot-2-
inch center who had the ability to maneuver and
score over bigger players. His high school teammates nicknamed him "Thomas Edison" for the
spectacular moves he invented.

A Philadelphia basketball legend, Monroe
can thank Leon Whitley for sending him to Winston-Salem State University. Whitley, a magnificent player at Philadelphia's Ben Franklin High
School in 1951, is a Winston-Salem Hall of Famer
honored not only for his stellar backcourt play,
but for sending such Philadelphians as Teddy
Blunt, Monroe and the Rev. George Gibson to
play for Hall of Famer Clarence "Big House"
Gaines.

Gaines had never seen Monroe before he arrived on campus. Whitley's word was good enough.

Monroe averaged 7.1, 23.2, 29.8 and 41.5 points in his four seasons at Winston-Salem. His 1,329 points as a Ram senior were a national record. He shot 16-for-30 for 40 points as Winston-Salem beat Southwest Missouri State, 77-74, in the NCAA College Division title game.

Monroe came to Winston-Salem as a deep shooter, but evolved into a magician who could mesmerize his way through traffic to score three points the old fashioned way, two plus one. He remains the most accomplished player and crowd attraction ever to attend a historically black college. Billy Packer used to come over from Wake Forest just to watch Monroe play.

"Winston-Salem was a good school for me," said Monroe. "I was able to play some good basketball and receive a fine education, too. It was a nice experience for me. I was away from home for four years and during that time I was able to learn a lot about life."

During his senior year, Monroe observed, "This year, I'm averaging 14 points more, but I'm making 70 percent of my shots. I'm learning to use picks and screens better.

"I take my time. I took a look at Oscar Robertson and Sam Jones. They're pretty cool. They don't let too much bother them and they don't

New York Knicks photo
Earl Monroe

have but 24 seconds before they have to shoot."

Detroit won a coin flip and made Jimmy Walker, Providence All-American guard, the No. 1 pick in the 1967 NBA draft. The Baltimore Bullets made Monroe the second pick. Monroe went on to become the Rookie of the Year, averaging 24.3 points a game in 1968.

In Baltimore, he played with Hall of Famer Wes Unseld, Jack Marin, Fred Carter, Kevin Loughery and Gus Johnson. Monroe entertained the fans with his double pump moves, spin dribbles, twisting and turning shots. He was the most exciting player in the league.

He spent the first four years of his NBA career with the Bullets. In 1971, Monroe was traded to the New York Knicks, where he teamed with Walt Frazier to form the league's finest backcourt. Monroe helped the Knicks win the NBA championship in 1973 with his razzle dazzle moves.

"Earl was probably the most entertaining player in the history of the game," said Red Holzman, Knicks head coach. "With his flair for doing the impossible game after game, Earl was one of the most complete and intelligent players I have ever coached."

Monroe not only entertained the fans in the NBA, but also in Philadelphia's Charles Baker Summer League. He developed the habit of arriving late, ducking his head through the door and prompting fans to pass the word along, "Magic is here...Magic is here...Magic is here." Sonny Hill, former CBS commentator, called Monroe "Mr. Baker League."

Monroe set a Baker League indoor scoring record of 64 points when his Gaddie Real Estate team defeated Willard Medics, 162-149, in overtime. However, many Baker League fans still talk about the night Monroe outgunned Bill Bradley 63-51 as Gaddie edged Jimmy Bates B-Bar in a playoff game.

Monroe, a four-time NBA all-star, retired in 1980. He had scored 17,454 points and dished out 3,594 assists in his 13 year career. He was elected to the NBA Hall of Fame in 1990 and is also a member of the Philadelphia Basketball Hall of Fame. Monroe resides in New York City, where he operates recording companies and has been an NBA broadcast analyst.

JOHN MCLENDON

John McLendon went straight to the source to learn about the game of basketball. As a student at the University of Kansas, McLendon learned the game from its inventor, Dr. James Naismith, a teacher and one-time coach at Kansas. He also came under the tutelage of legendary Kansas basketball coach "Phog" Allen. He then used that knowledge to become the first coach to win three straight national championships.

McLendon coached Tennessee State to the 1957, 1958 and 1959 NAIA national titles. His ballclubs were noted for outstanding defense, a lightening-quick fast-break offense and well-conditioned athletes. He brought exposure to black college basketball and helped to start an era of

John McLendon, right, is honored during a CIAA awards ceremony. Making the presentation is Dr. Leroy Walker, president of the United States Olympic Committee and former track coach at North Carolina Central University. (Photo courtesy CIAA)

integrated basketball. McLendon coached on all levels of the game.

"John has served with distinction as a successful coach on the high school, college, AAU and professional levels," said Clarence "Big House" Gaines, former head coach at Winston-

Salem State University. "His contributions to basketball over his years have been meritorious. He is a scholar, sportsman, gentleman and recognized as the father of black basketball."

Gaines credits much of what he knows to McLendon.

"He was truly ahead of his time," Gaines said. "He's done it all. If you ever have a question about basketball, just ask John McLendon. He knows about zone and man-to-man defenses, fast breaks, halfcourt play — you name it."

Because major universities had not yet broken the color barrier, McLendon was never able to play basketball as a student at Kansas. In 1936, however, he became the first black to earn a degree in the school's physical education program.

He coached Sam Jones, ex-Boston Celtics great at North Carolina College and former New York Knicks shooting guard Dick Barnett at Tennessee State. Jones and Barnett were two of the NBA's finest players.

McLendon coached North Carolina College, Hampton, Tennessee State, Kentucky State and Cleveland State along with the Cleveland Pipers (NBL-ABL) and the Denver Rockets of the American Basketball Association (ABA). His teams won a combined 523 games and McLendon put together a 76 percent winning record over his 25-year career.

In 1958, he was named NAIA Coach of the Year. He coached teams that captured eight Central Intercollegiate Athletic Association championships between 1941 and 1952, the NBL and AAU championships in 1961, and the ABL Eastern Division crown in 1962.

McLendon also served as a State Department basketball specialist to Southeast Asia and as a consultant to the Virgin Islands and Bahamas basketball federations. In 1964 he coached the NAIA Olympic Trials team and in 1973 he coached a team representing the United States in the World Basketball Festival in Lima, Peru. He received a special award for the development of international basketball in 1976.

McLendon has authored two books, *Fast Break Basketball* and *The Fast Break Game*. He has been involved with basketball more than 60 years and in 1978 was elected to the Naismith Basketball Hall of Fame. He also is a member of the Helms Hall of Fame and the CIAA Hall of Fame.

EDWIN MOSES

When Edwin Moses came to Morehouse College in Atlanta, Ga., it wasn't because of his magnificent running skills. Moses, a native of Dayton, Ohio, went to college on an academic scholarship and majored in physics.

Morehouse did not have a track, so he prepared for the 1976 Olympic Trials at public high school facilities in Atlanta. The physics major secured a spot on the 1976 U.S. Olympic track team and in the 1976 games set a world record of 47.64 seconds in winning in the 400-meter hurdles.

"I suppose I was the most unlikely person to go to the Olympics — a physics major from a small school with no track at the time," Moses said. "But at Morehouse, I had the inspiration

Edwin Moses went to Morehouse College to major in phys-ics before becoming an Olympic champion in the 400-meter hurdles. (Photo by Tony Duffy, ©All-Sport USA, Inc.)

of students and administrators who rallied around me. I would not have gone to the Olympics if I had not come from Morehouse."

For more than 10 years, he remained unbeaten in the 400-meter hurdles by developing a 13-step method that proved to be very successful. His smooth stride kept him in rhythm throughout the race, and his great endurance allowed him to outlast his opponents.

He was favored to win the 400-meter hurdles in 1980, but the United States boycotted the Olympics in Moscow. In 1984, he won another gold medal at the Olympics in Los Angeles and had won 107 consecutive races before silver medalist Danny Harris upset him at a race in Madrid.

Moses was able to amass 10 more consecutive wins, for a total of 117 victories in 119 starts. But he was getting older, and in the 1988 Olympic Games in Seoul, South Korea, he finished behind teammate Andre Phillips and silver medalist El Hedji Dia Ba of Senegal. Moses completed his track and field career that year. His best time in the 400-meter hurdles was 47.02.

A true competitor, however, Moses became a member of the U.S. World Championship Bobsled Team in 1991. His team won the bronze medal in the two-man sled in the Winter Olympics at Winterberg, Germany.

In 1994, Moses was inducted into the United States Track and Field Hall of Fame. That same year, he earned a master's degree in business management from Pepperdine University. In 1996, he was inducted into the Southern Intercollegiate Athletic Conference Hall of Fame.

Also in 1996, Moses was honored by his alma mater, Morehouse College by the placement of a bronze marker on the plaza of the school's B.T. Harvey Stadium/Edwin C. Moses Track commemorating his athletic achievements.

"I've had a lot of big days with the Olympics, but this is right up there with the best of them," Moses told the Associated Press during the ceremony, which also marked the 20th anniversary of his first gold medal-winning performance. "This recognition is like getting another gold medal."

Currently a financial consultant with Robinson-Humphrey Company, Inc., an investment banking firm and subsidiary of Smith Barney Inc., Moses continues to be a part of the Olympic Games in a noncompetitive role. At the 1996 Games held in Atlanta, Moses was honored by being selected as a bearer of the Olympic flag at the opening ceremonies of the Games.

Wilma Rudolph

If any youngster needs a source of inspiration to overcome huge obstacles in life, he or she should look at Wilma Rudolph.

Born in Bethlehem, Tenn., Rudolph had battled scarlet fever, double pneumonia and polio all by the time she was 4 years old. But she never gave up.

Polio cost her the use of her left leg and she had to wear a huge brace. Her mother and father, Blanche and Ed Rudolph, refused to believe that she would never walk. They gave her daily massages and exercise to help improve her physical condition.

When Rudolph was 8 years old, she was able to take the brace off and use an orthopedic left

Wilma Rudolph overcame polio to win gold medals in the Olympics. (Photo courtesy of Tennessee State University)

shoe. And when she turned 12 she was able to play basketball without the use of her orthopedic shoe.

At 16, Rudolph became a great high school basketball player. Her terrific speed on the basketball court prompted coaches to encourage her to participate in track.

In the 1956 Olympics, Rudolph traveled to Australia and won a bronze medal in the 400-meter relay. Known in Europe as the "Black Gazelle," Rudolph made history at the 1960 Games in Rome, becoming the first American woman

Wilma Rudolph won three gold medals at the 1960 Olympics in Rome. In 1962 she was recognized as the top woman athlete in the world. (Photo courtesy United States Olympic Committee)

After battling polio as a child, Wilma Rudolph earned a bronze medal in the 1956 Olympics. She followed that by winning three gold medals in the 1960 Games. (Photo courtesy United States Olympic Committee)

to win three gold medals in a single Olympiad. She won gold medals in the 100-meter dash in 11.0 seconds and won the 200 meters in an Olympic record time of 23.2 seconds. She also anchored the world-record-setting 400-meter relay team in a time of 44.4 seconds.

She was voted Woman Athlete of the Year and Sportsman of the Year by European writers. The Associated Press selected Rudolph as Female Athlete of the Year in 1960 and 1961. She was invited to compete in a number of previously all-male meets, such as the New York Athletic Club meet and the Milrose Games.

After being recognized as the top woman athlete in the world in 1962, Rudolph finished her track career at Stanford against the Soviet Union, winning the 100 and 200 meters while receiving a standing ovation.

Before she became an Olympic hero, Rudolph displayed her skills for Ed Temple's Tennessee State University Tiger Belles. Rudolph, nicknamed "Skeeter" by her friends, produced three first-place finishes at the 1960 AAU national indoor meet in Chicago.

In 1962, she founded the Wilma Rudolph Foundation, a nonprofit community-based amateur sports program aimed at the development of neighborhood track teams and international-caliber athletes.

In 1980, Rudolph was a charter inductee in the Women's Sports Foundation's Women's Sports Hall of Fame. She was inducted into the Olympic Hall of Fame in 1983. In 1987, she was one of five athletes to receive the NCAA's Silver Anniversary Award for distinguished careers and lives after sports over a 25-year period. Her autobiography, *Wilma*, was published in 1977 and later produced by NBC as a two-hour documentary.

Rudolph, who died in 1994, should be remembered as a young person who overcame major physical problems and gained success on and off the field.

ALTHEA GIBSON

In 1957, Althea Gibson, a shining star of Florida A&M's tennis program, became the first African-American woman to win a singles title at Wimbledon.

Gibson, a 5-foot-10-inch, 165-pounder, was the holder of the National Negro Women's singles title since 1947. In 1950, she became the first black to compete in the United States National singles championship at Forest Hills, New York, reaching the second round in her first attempt. Between 1950 and 1957, she won numerous international tennis tournaments, including the French Open championship in 1956.

Using the French Open championship as a springboard into the 1957 season, Gibson scored

Althea Gibson prepares to make a forehand shot during her tennis playing days. In 1957, Gibson became the first black woman to win a singles title at Wimbledon. (Photo courtesy International Tennis Hall of Fame)

her first major United States tennis victory, defeating Darlene Hard in the National Clay Court championships. That same year, she captured the first of two straight U.S. Open women's titles at Forest Hills and started a string of two straight championships at Wimbledon.

The Associated Press named her the 1957-58 Woman Athlete of the Year. Gibson also won the prestigious Babe Zaharias Award, which is presented to the top female athlete.

Proving that she was not a one-sport athlete, Gibson joined the Ladies Professional Golf Association (LPGA) tour in 1963, breaking ground for the entry of blacks into this lucractive sports profession.

Gibson, the eldest of Daniel and Anna (Washington) Gibson's five children, was reared in the Harlem area of New York City. She played paddle tennis on a Police Athletic League "play street." Later she entered Park Department tennis and won the Manhattan girls' championship. Introduced in 1942 to the interracial Cosmopolitan Tennis Club by Buddy Walker, a band leader who was also a PAL play street supervisor, she was coached there by Fred Johnson.

In 1943, she won the New York State Negro girls' singles championship. Dr. H.A. Eaton, a black physician and tennis enthusiast, invited Gibson to stay with his family while attending the Industrial High School at Wilmington, North Carolina.

Today, Gibson resides in East Orange, New Jersey. She was recently inducted into the Southern Intercollegiate Athletic Conference Hall of Fame.

ALICE COACHMAN

(DAVIS)

The first black woman to win an Olympic gold medal, Alice Coachman made history at the 1948 Games in London. Coachman capped a 10-year career by setting an Olympic women's high jump record of 5 feet, 6 inches. Hers was the only title by the United States women's track and field team.

Coachman, a former track and field standout at Tuskegee Institute, not only became the first of only three American Olympic women high jump champions since 1928, but established an Olympic record that stood for eight years. Moreover, Coachman achieved that mark on her first attempt at that height.

She won 10 consecutive U.S. high jump titles, along with national titles at 50 meters, 100

Alice Coachman Davis shows the gold medal she won in the high jump at the 1948 Olympics. (Photo courtesy Alice Coachman Track and Field Foundation)

meters and the 400-meter relay. Overall, she won 34 American titles — 23 individually, four in relay events and seven as a member of the Tuskegee Institute National Championship Teams.

"I really enjoyed participating in track and field at Tuskegee," Coachman said. "I competed against some of the best athletes in the country."

Coachman credits much of her success in the Tuskegee program to track and field coach Cleve Abbott.

"Cleve was a very knowledgeable coach and did an outstanding job of coaching me at Tuskegee," she said. "We won a lot of championships with him."

Coachman would have contended for Olympic medals before 1948 had not World War II forced the cancellation of the 1940 and 1944

Alice Coachman Davis was 25 years old before she finally got to participate in the Olympics. In the 1948 Games, she won the only gold medal among U.S. women. (Photo courtesy United States Olympic Committee)

Summer Games. She didn't get the opportunity to participate in the Olympics until the age of 25.

Albany State coach and athletic director Christopher Roulhac Jr. was Coachman's Olympic coach.

"I was well-prepared for the Olympics thanks to Dr. Roulhac," Coachman said. "He had me competing against the best athletes.

"Because he worked with me on the fundamentals of high jumping I felt I had a big edge on all the other athletes. I really enjoyed my experience at both Albany State and Tuskegee. They're two fine schools."

Her fame allowed her to become the first black female athlete to endorse an international product when Coca-Cola signed her to a contract to endorse the beverage in 1952. This opened the door for future endorsement opportunities for outstanding black women athletes such as Jackie Joyner Kersee, Evelyn Ashford and Florence Griffith Joyner.

Following her retirement from track, Coachman earned her B.S. degree from Albany State College, and became a teacher and track and field coach.

In 1994, she started the Alice Coachman Track and Field Foundation, a nonprofit organization which assists young athletes as they pursue their dreams of becoming Olympic champions and former Olympians as they make their transition to life after athletics. Nellie Gordon Roulhac recently authored a book on Coachman's career, *Jumping Over The Moon*.

She was inducted into the Southern Intercollegiate Athletic Conference Hall of Fame in 1996 and was honored as one of the 100 greatest Olympic athletes at the 1996 Olympics in Atlanta.

Married to Frank A. Davis and the mother of two children, she currently resides in Tuskegee, Alabama, where she attended high school and began her college studies.

ART SHELL

During his 15-year career from 1968 to 1982 with the Oakland/Los Angeles Raiders, Art Shell became widely recognized as the NFL's premier offensive left tackle. The 6-foot-5, 285-pound Shell was considered by many pro football experts to be the most outstanding among the linemen who played for the Raiders.

Shell's size made him ideal for an offensive tackle. But he also combined a delicate balance of speed and agility, pride and dignity, along with brains and strength. For most of his career, he teamed with left guard Gene Upshaw to form such a lethal blocking unit that one opponent ruefully commented: "The two of them block out the sun!"

After a standout career as a football and basketball player at Maryland State, now Maryland-Eastern Shore, Art Shell was drafted by the Oakland Raiders and played on two Super Bowl champion teams. (Photo courtesy Kansas City Chiefs)

When Oakland coaches reviewed game films each week, Shell received consistently high grades but he reached his zenith in Super Bowl XI when the Raiders routed the Minnesota Vikings, 32-14. In the first half alone, the Raiders aimed 27 of 33 running plays toward two all-stars, Alan Page and Jim Marshall, on the right side of Minnesota's defensive front.

Shell and Upshaw paved the way for a then-record 266-yard rushing output with crushing blocks. Marshall, Shell's primary blocking target, had no tackles and no assists, a completely lost day.

"When somebody told me I had a perfect game, I was shocked," Shell said. "I was too busy to keep track. Play by play, quarter by quarter, I was totally involved in doing the best job I could."

"The best I could" was basically the way Shell played throughout his career. While he was often overshadowed by the more flamboyant Upshaw, who became the unofficial spokesman for a generation of Raider linemen, Shell definitely made his own mark on the National Football League scene.

Equally adept as a pass protector or as a blocker on running plays, Shell was an All-AFC selection from 1973 through 1978 and All-Pro in 1973, 1974 and 1978. Shell played in eight Pro Bowls and 24 postseason contests, including eight AFL/AFC championship games and the Raiders' victories in Super Bowl XI and XV.

Shell played in his first 156 pro games before a preseason injury in 1979 forced him out of the lineup for five games. He then launched another streak of 51 games that was finally aborted by injuries midway through his final 1982 campaign. Altogether, he played in 207 regular-season games. Upshaw and Shell are the only Raiders whose careers spanned parts of three decades.

"I was fortunate in the sense of never having a serious injury," said Shell, who was elected to the Pro Football Hall of Fame in 1989. "I never had an operation. You have to be lucky and you have to play hard."

Shell's work ethic and his complete dedication to the total team effort earned him the tremendous respect of teammates and opponents alike.

"He was one of those quiet leaders who commanded respect just by being a great player," said former Raiders coach John Madden. "He never, ever acted like a tough guy. He was always nice and business-like. But whether you were his teammate or an opponent, you knew this was a man who deserved respect."

When Shell was playing football in high school and college, he was continually reprimanded for not being mean enough.

"I thought I was doing well," Shell remembered, "but the coaches thought I would do a whole lot better if I were mean. I'm just not a mean person."

Shell was born in Charleston, S.C. His mother died when he was 10 and he was raised by his father. Since his father worked long hours at a paper mill, Shell, as the oldest of five children, had to look after the rest of the kids.

"We never gave our parents a bad time," Shell said. "Our mother taught us well when she was with us. Then when she wasn't there anymore, we just had to carry on. We were very, very close to our father. He talked softly, but when he said something, you knew he meant it. When he did pull out the rod, you knew you deserved it and you were awfully sorry."

His father, who died the same year Shell was notified of his selection to the Hall of Fame, gave him a strong sense of responsibility.

At Bonds-Wilson High School in North Charleston, Shell was an all-state star in football and basketball. He was thinking of going to Grambling when the Maryland State football coach showed up at his house and insisted, "I'm not leaving without you."

Shell knew it would be too much of a burden for his father to pay for his college education so Maryland State (now Maryland-Eastern Shore) it was.

At Maryland State, Shell played both football and basketball. For the first two years on the gridiron, Shell was a center and defensive tackle, but he spent his last two years as a two-way tackle. He was all-conference three years, All-America two years on the *Pittsburgh Courier* and *Ebony* magazine teams and little All-America as a senior in 1967.

The Raiders selected him in the third round of the combined AFL-NFL draft in 1968. "The primary thing we saw in Art was his great size," Madden said.

"But we also were excited that he was an accomplished basketball player. With that size, combined with his ability to move his feet and the agility he showed on the basketball court, we knew we had a quality prospect."

Shell played behind veteran lineman Bob Svihus for two seasons. But in 1970, Svihus was injured giving Shell his chance.

"I want to start. I'll give it everything I've got," Shell said. "I don't know if I can hold the job, but I do know the best man will win it."

Shell did prevail and, except when he was injured, he never sat on the bench again. After injury-free seasons, most of them as a starter, Shell was carried from the field with a damaged knee in the 1979 preseason. He was 32 years old and many thought his career might be over. But once again Shell proved the value of hard work. By the beginning of October, just seven weeks later, Shell was back on the field harassing defensive ends.

"It was an amazing recovery," Raiders coach Tom Flores said. "He worked out as many as four times a day on his own. Any other player would have been out for the season."

Throughout Shell's career, his weight remained a mystery. Early in his tenure, the Raiders press book listed his weight at 255 and then at 265. By 1981 and 1982, his published weight was established at 285 pounds. Some, however, guessed he was closer to 300, possibly even as high as 320 pounds.

"John Madden told me as long as I performed it didn't matter to him how much I weighed, so when everybody else got on the scales, I would walk by," Shell said. "But I will tell you honestly the day when I weighed the most. It was the day of Super Bowl XI. I went into the locker room alone and weighed myself just before the game — I weighed 310 pounds."

In 1989, Los Angeles Raiders president Al Davis made Shell the first black head coach in the modern NFL. During his six seasons (1989-94) as Raiders head coach, he compiled a record of 54-38 and guided his club to three playoff appearances.

After taking over the 1-3 Raiders in '89, he led the club to a 7-5 mark in his first 12 games as head coach. He captured the AFC West title with a 12-4 record in '90 when he was named Coach of the Year by UPI, *The Sporting News* and *Football News*, and also coached the AFC to a win in the Pro Bowl following the '90 campaign. His clubs went 9-7 in '91 and 7-9 in '92, in addition to a 10-6 mark in '93 and a 9-7 record in '94.

Shell is currently in his second year as the Kansas City Chiefs offensive line coach.

LEM BARNEY

Lem Barney took the National Football League by storm when he joined the Detroit Lions as their second-round pick in 1967. The 6-foot, 190-pound speedster from Jackson State came out of his first pro football training camp as the starting left cornerback.

In the 1967 season opener against the Super Bowl champion Green Bay Packers, he intercepted the first pass Bart Starr threw into his territory, did a somersault, regained his footing and scooted 24 yards for a touchdown. In the season finale against Minnesota, Barney swiped three passes in one quarter. He took one of them 71 yards for a touchdown.

Barney wound up the season tied with David Whitsell of New Orleans for the NFL intercep-

tion title with 10. He returned three interceptions for touchdowns, a rookie feat matched only
by Ronnie Lott of San Francisco. Barney permit-
ted only one touchdown the entire season.

In a runaway vote, Barney was named the
Associated Press Defensive Rookie of the Year.
He was also selected to some All-Pro teams and
named to play in his first Pro Bowl.

Barney played with distinction for 10 more
seasons with the Lions. He was one of history's
premier cornerbacks and also excelled as a punt
and kickoff return specialist.

Had certain members of the Detroit staff
prevailed, however, Barney would never have
become a Lion. His credentials were good —
three-time All-Southwestern Athletic Conference
with 26 interceptions at Jackson State. He also
could run the 100 yards in 9.7 seconds. Still,
some doubted if he could have learned enough
in a small black college to make it in the NFL.

But new coach Joe Schmidt recognized that
the Lions were in desperate need of a cornerback
to replace Dick "Night Train" Lane, the future
Hall of Famer who had retired in 1965. Barney
was strongly recommended by Lions scout Will
Robinson.

The Lions went to the touted UCLA running back, Mel Farr, in the first round and then
tapped Barney in the second round.

©Detroit Lions

Lem Barney

Farr, who became Barney's roommate as a rookie, had the big-school "smarts" to employ an agent who got him a big signing bonus. Barney had no agent and settled for a three-year deal for $15,000 his rookie season, $16,000 in 1968 and $17,000 in 1969. He felt he was just lucky to have the chance to play pro football.

Schmidt was quite certain his new cornerback would not play as much as a rookie. "Pretty damn slight," he answered when a reporter asked about Barney's chances of starting in 1967. "It takes a little longer to learn how to play cornerback than almost any other position."

Barney wasn't invited to play in the College All-Star game and this proved to be a big break because it gave him an opportunity to prove his mettle in the early days of his summer grind.

Defensive coach Jim David, who had been an outstanding safety in the Lions' championship years of the 1950s, pitted Barney against Gale Cogdill, a former All-Pro receiver, in the first camp scrimmage. Barney deflected the first pass thrown to Cogdill and made a one-armed interception on the second.

Cogdill screamed: "That's interference," but Barney cockily retorted: "Offensive or defensive?" The rookie cornerback was well on the way to proving he belonged.

Barney was not a violent player. He preferred to level his opponents with a leg tackle instead of with a more vicious shoulder-high "clothesline" stop. And he always offered a helping hand to those he knocked down. One such tackle of Gale Sayers, of Chicago, he yanked his opponent up and then shook his hand.

"That was our fraternity grip," said Barney, who was inducted into the Pro Football Hall of Fame in 1992. "We both were in Kappa Alpha Psi when we were in college. But don't tell the coach. He might not like me fraternizing with the enemy."

Detroit was perennially beset with offensive problems and Schmidt was often asked if Barney might be more valuable on offense.

"The best athletes you have on the team play at cornerback," the coach replied. "The receivers come at you one-on-one and you just can't hide. You either make the play or you don't. It's that simple. Barney makes plays because of his speed, his quickness, his reactions, his senses."

*Lem Barney breaks up another pass during his NFL career
with the Detroit Lions. (Photo © Detroit Lions)*

It seemed that everything came easily for Barney. There were touchdowns galore, All-Pro honors, the Pro Bowl. There were kick returns when he zigzagged through 11 tacklers, outran them and then waved back at his frustrated pursuers as he neared the goal line. He was even popular — a real morale-booster — with his teammates. For Lem Barney in the late 1960s, pro football was a lark.

But in 1970, he was awarded a handsome $42,000 contract that made him the highest-paid cornerback in the NFL. He had two Pro Bowl seasons in 1975 and 1976, and finished his career in Detroit in 1977.

Barney, who played in seven Pro Bowls and was named All-Pro three times, became recognized as Detroit's "offense on defense." He scored 10 touchdowns, seven on interceptions, two on punt returns, one on a kickoff return and seven of his defensive touchdowns came on plays of 40 yards or more. In one four-game stretch in 1968, the Lions scored only two touchdowns, both of them by Barney.

With his interceptions and returns, he accumulated 3,972 yards. He had 56 interceptions, tying him for 11th in NFL history, for 1,079 yards. He netted 1,312 yards on 143 punt returns and added 1,274 yards on kickoff returns.

Barney, a native of Gulfport, Miss., played quarterback on the 33rd Avenue High School football team. On Sundays, he watched NFL football and studied quarterbacks on black-and-white television.

"As I got older, I rooted for Y.A. Tittle and Johnny Unitas," he recalls.

When it came time for college, Barney was not heavily recruited. His mother urged him to give college a try for at least one year so he went to Jackson State.

"I recognized that there was no demand for black quarterbacks in the pros back in 1967," Barney says, "So I asked my coach, Rod Paige, to change me into a defensive back."

In the NFL, Barney had to settle for individual acclaim for he never played in a playoff game, let alone win a championship or appear in a Super Bowl. He played under four different head coaches with the Lions, who finished above .500 just four times in his 11 seasons.

"I never had a chance to be a champion in football or basketball from the sandlots to college and on to the pros," said Barney, who now is a public relations counselor for Michigan Consolidated Gas Co. in the Detroit area and is also a football commentator for Black Entertainment Television network.

"Now I feel like I am a champion," he said after being inducted into the Pro Football Hall of Fame.

WALTER PAYTON

If you're a Chicago Bears fan, then you probably remember names like Gale Sayers, Dick Butkus and Mike Singletary. But if you're a true Bears fan, one name you'll never forget is Walter Payton.

In 13 seasons with the Bears from 1975 to 1987, Payton rewrote the NFL record book with his running talents. He rushed 3,838 times for 16,726 yards and 110 touchdowns — all records. He also caught 492 passes for 4,538 yards and 15 more touchdowns. Altogether, he scored 125 touchdowns, second-highest ever, and accounted for a record 21,803 combined net yards.

Payton rushed for an all-time high 275 yards against Minnesota on November 20, 1977. He rushed for more than 100 yards 77 times. He won the NFL kickoff return championship as a rookie, and even completed 11 of 34 passes for 331 yards and eight touchdowns. No other running back has even remotely threatened Payton's overall production.

Chicago Bears photo
Walter Payton

Payton's exceptional rushing statistics tend to obscure the fact that he was an exceptional all-around football player blessed with a wide variety of athletic skills which he put to good use.

"He is a complete football player," Jim Finks, the Chicago Bears general manager who drafted Payton, said, "He is better than Jim Brown. He is better than O.J. Simpson."

Payton prided himself on his blocking ability. One of his fondest memories drifts back to 1985 when he intercepted a blitzing Minnesota linebacker to make it possible for Jim McMahon to throw a crucial touchdown pass.

"Walter takes pride in the little things, the blocking, the faking," said former Bears coach Mike Ditka. "Once against Cincinnati, he picked up a couple of linebackers and liked to have killed them."

Payton played football with "the enthusiasm of a 10th-grader trying to be the best tailback on the team," teammate Dan Hampton once said. He trained tirelessly by weight lifting and jogging during every off-season and always appeared at training camp in top shape. He missed only one game, in 1975, in his first 12 seasons.

Payton suffered bumps and bruises, but he never let it bother him. When he had arthroscopic surgery on both knees after the 1983 season, Payton referred to it merely as "my 11,000-yard checkup."

Payton's running style was unusual in that his knees rarely bent when he ran. Most running backs flex their knees at least twice as much. Payton's leg swing came from the hips instead, thus giving him more power and extra leverage and shifting the burden of running to the upper leg and off the knees, the most vulnerable joints.

His relatively straight-legged motion made it easier for Payton to run on his toes, for the ordinary player a nearly impossible task. Payton was inordinately strong in his thighs, hamstrings and buttocks making him more of a power runner than a breakaway speedster.

A native of Columbia, Miss., Payton was the youngest and the shyest of three children. His father, a factory worker, played semipro baseball, but Walter described himself as a "Mama's boy."

His mother often made trips to Chicago to see her boy play.

Payton thrived in the classroom but music was as much a part of his life as organized sports.

"My cymbal playing is one thing I'll brag about," he once said. "Man, I was good."

Also a great dancer, Walter once made the national contest finals of TV's *Soul Train*.

Payton did not play football until his junior year in high school. He ran 65 yards for a touchdown on his first high school carry and scored on a 75-yard play later the same game.

He was avidly recruited by major colleges but enrolled at Jackson State so he could play in the same backfield as his older brother, Edward, now the highly successful golf coach at Jackson State.

He rushed for 3,563 yards in four seasons at Jackson State and scored an NCAA record 464 points on 66 touchdowns, five field goals and 53 extra points. It was in college that Payton picked up his famous nickname, "Sweetness," because of the smooth way he ran.

Payton was the Bears' first choice in the 1975 draft. The Bears had gone a long time without a championship and Chicago rooters saw Payton as a savior. He was immediately compared to Gale Sayers, who had terrorized NFL defenses in the 1960s.

Walter Payton set numerous records during his career with the Chicago Bears. (Photo courtesy Chicago Bears)

"If the people of Chicago give me some time and are patient, I'll give them a new Gale Sayers," Payton promised. "No running back patterns himself after anybody. It's something that is innate. It's reflexes and instinct."

Payton reported to rookie camp with a sore elbow he received in the College All-Star game and he missed the 1975 preseason. In the season opener, he was held to no yards rushing on eight carries. Still, he wound up the season with 679 yards, the most yards for a Bear since Sayers in 1969, and led the NFL in kickoff returns. Yet he was not named to the NFL All-Rookie team. Payton was disappointed, not for himself, but for his team.

"He thinks he has to carry the Bears on his shoulders," said Bears coach Jack Pardee. "He has a great sense of loyalty."

Payton returned in 1976 determined to breathe fire into the Bears. He had hyperventilated, suffered nausea, headaches and dizziness in preseason games and doctors warned him he was too intense, that he should loosen up.

But it came together for Payton that year. He led the NFC with 1,390 yards and 13 touchdowns. He was an All-Pro and appeared in his first of nine Pro Bowls. In 1977, he recorded a career-high 1,852 yards, and scored an NFL-leading 16 touchdowns and 92 points.

He rushed for more than 1,000 yards in 10 of 13 seasons, won one NFL and five NFC rushing titles, and was named All-Pro five consecutive years from 1976 through 1980 and four more times from 1983 through 1986. He was selected as the NFL's Most Valuable Player in 1977 and again in 1985, and was the NFC Player of the Year three times.

Still, there was one big thing missing from Payton's football life — a championship. The Bears won the 1984 NFC Central championship but were beaten in the NFC championship game by the San Francisco 49ers, 23-0, although Payton rushed for 92 yards.

The next year, the Bears rolled to a 15-1 record, then defeated the Los Angeles Rams, 24-0, for the NFC championship. Payton had a banner season with 1,551 yards rushing and 483 yards on 49 pass receptions.

The Bears overwhelmed the New England Patriots, 46-10 in Super Bowl XX. Payton was the game's leading rusher with 61 yards on 22 carries, but was denied the chance to score a Super Bowl touchdown. With the ball on the Patriots' 1-yard line late in the game, Dikta called on William "Refrigerator" Perry to carry the ball.

"I knew I was going to be a decoy today and I was prepared for it," Payton commented after the game.

Payton broke Jim Brown's all-time rushing record of 12,312 yards in 1985.

"Brown set his record in nine seasons," Payton said. "I wish I could have done it in nine. I could have, too, if the strike hadn't shortened the 1982 season."

Payton, who retired after the 1987 season, was determined that his new rushing record would be something for the ages.

"My father always told me never to settle for second-best," he said, "that you either try to do your best or don't try at all."

Payton lived by his father's words and always gave 100 percent.

JOHN CHANEY

John Chaney is one of a handful of basketball head coaches to go from a historically black college to a Division I school. Chaney had a 225-59 record in 10 years at Cheyney State College in Cheyney, Pa. In 1978, he led Cheyney State to the NCAA Division II championship.

Peter Liacouras, Temple University president, wanted someone to build the Owls' basketball program into a national powerhouse and boost enrollment. Liacouras knew that man was John Chaney, who is known for holding 5:30 a.m. practices, which allow the players to get up early, eat breakfast and go to class without basketball on their minds.

In 1982, Chaney took over an Owls' basketball program that hadn't won an NCAA Tourna-

Photo courtesy Temple University

John Chaney

ment game since 1958. That first year at Temple was his most difficult, due to an early-season injury to Granger Hall. Nevertheless, Chaney still guided the Owls to a 14-15 record, including upsets over St. Joseph's and Rutgers in the first Atlantic 10 Conference tournament at the Spectrum.

"I was very fortunate that Peter Liacouras gave me an opportunity," Chaney said. "I was very happy at Cheyney State. I wasn't looking to go anywhere, but this was a good opportunity for me. If it wasn't for him, I don't know if I would ever have been able to coach at a school like Temple."

Chaney said he was lucky that someone like Liacouras noticed him and his accomplishments. It doesn't always happen that way for other black coaches.

"Black colleges have always had great coaches over the years," he said. "But in order for them to move up to major Division I schools, the presidents and athletic directors will have to give them a chance. During my career at Cheyney, I won a national championship, coach of the year, teacher of the year and never received an interview until Temple called."

The decision to hire Chaney turned out to be worthwhile for Temple. Only six schools have more victories than Temple's total of 1,455 —

North Carolina, Kentucky, Kansas, St. John's, Oregon State and Duke.

Under Chaney, the Owls are a mainstay on national television. They bring in players from all over and play the toughest nonconference schedule every year.

Here are some of Chaney's highlights with the Owls:

- Temple has played in 12 NCAA tournaments and in 13 straight postseason tournaments.

- Temple has won 16 NCAA games and three times — in 1988, 1991 and 1993 — advanced to a regional final.

- Temple had a stretch from 1983-88 when it won 25 or more games each year, winning 140 and losing just 23.

- Temple has won four Atlantic 10 regular-season titles (in 1986, 1987, 1988, 1990) and four A-10 tournament championships (in 1985, '87, '88 and '90).

- Temple has won or shared 10 Philadelphia Big 5 titles. The 1988 Owls are the only Philadelphia team to be ranked No. 1 in the polls.

Chaney, 64, has twice been honored as national coach of the year. During the 1986-87 season the United States Basketball Writers Association unanimously selected Chaney for the honor following Temple's 32-4 season. The following year the Associated Press, United Press International, CNN/*USA Today*, U.S.B.W.A., Kodak and Chevrolet panels selected Chaney as its top coach making him that year's national consensus coach of the year. That year he led the Owls to their best-ever 32-2 season and Temple was ranked No. 1 in the final polls. He won another coach of the year award with Cheyney State in 1978.

Chaney is the fourth-winningest active Division I men's basketball coach. His 24-year collegiate record stands at 540-188.

"I've been very fortunate to have some great players and coaches with me over the years," Chaney said. "I think most of the kids who played for me whether you're talking Cheyney State or Temple have given me a maximum effort. I mean, these kids want to win and excel off and on the court."

That's something that Alvin Gentry, an assistant coach with the Detroit Pistons has noticed in kids who have come out of the Temple program.

"You see those people out of John Chaney's program at Temple and you know they have the whole package," said Gentry. "Eddie Jones of the Lakers showed us that, and now you can see that

Aaron McKie is cut from the same mold — a good defender, a smart player who uses good judgment, good fundamentals, good shooting.

"You watch these guys over the years and you know that they're going to come into the league a little ahead of the other rookies."

Chaney measures his success with his teams not only in wins and losses, but in life after college. While he can rejoice in the accomplishments some of his players have achieved in the NBA, his message for his players is that an education is the most important thing. A winning attitude can help you find that success in or out of athletics.

"I've always wanted to provide our kids with an opportunity to play basketball and receive a good education," Chaney said. "This way, they can become successful. That's what makes a strong program. Winning is an attitude."

Chaney was a great basketball player, too. In 1951, he played for Philadelphia's Ben Franklin High School, where he was named Public League Player of the Year. Chaney played his college basketball at Bethune-Cookman College, where he was named an NAIA All-American in 1953.

"It was a good experience for me," Chaney said of his playing days at Bethune-Cookman. "I traveled to a number of cities in the South that had black colleges. Bethune-Cookman played just about everybody down there."

Chaney said the level of competition at black colleges was excellent when he was playing. One of his opponents was Tennessee State's Dick Barnett, who went on to become an outstanding guard for New York Knicks in the NBA.

"He (Barnett) could have played for anyone," Chaney said.

Immediately following his college career, he played 11 years of professional basketball in the old Eastern League from 1955-1966. He also coached in the Eastern Basketball League. He coached Kent Taverneers (with Hal Greer and Chet Walker) to five straight titles in the Charles Baker Summer League.

EDDIE ROBINSON

Eddie Robinson, Grambling State University's legendary football coach, believes everybody should give credit where credit is due. However, he doesn't like to take credit for himself, for his great success at Grambling and for providing hundreds of kids with an opportunity to succeed in life.

He says his players, his family, his loyal wife Doris, the sportswriters and the loyal fans around the country have all helped in making the name Eddie Robinson well-known in the sports world.

Robinson enters each new season with the same enthusiasm and energy that he had when he started coaching in 1941. He still rings the bell each day to wake people up in the dormitory.

Legendary Grambling coach Eddie Robinson sits with some of the many trophies and awards he's won during a career that's spanned more than 50 years. (Photo courtesy Grambling State University)

"Nobody has ever done or ever will do what Eddie Robinson has done for this game," Penn State's Joe Paterno said. "Eddie Robinson and Jake Gaither (Florida A&M) stand alone. Our profession will never, ever be able to repay Eddie Robinson for what he has done for the country and the profession of football."

Robinson, who fielded his 53rd Grambling team (no team two years because of World II) in 1996, has been inducted into the NAIA, Sugar

Bowl, Pop Warner, Louisiana Sports, Southwestern Athletic Conference and Grambling halls of fame. In 1995, he won his 400th game when his Grambling Tigers defeated Mississippi Valley State University, 42-6. Robinson has developed some magnificent players over the years such as Doug Williams, Jake Reed, Sammie White, Charlie Joiner, Tank Younger, Willie Brown, Willie Davis and Buck Buchanan.

"Means can be justifiable in the end," Robinson said. "The football players are the most important people in the world to me. Without them there would be no me."

Immediately after graduating from now-defunct Leland College of Baton Rouge, La., in 1941, Robinson came to Grambling. He has since guided the once-obscure Tigers to national and international popularity. His teams have played in almost every major city in the United States and was the first U.S. collegiate team to play in Japan in 1976. The school has sent more than 300 players to pro camps, including 200 who have made NFL rosters.

Grambling got its first national attention in 1949 when Paul "Tank" Younger signed with the Los Angeles Rams, becoming the first player from a historically black college to be taken by the NFL. Robinson's teams have won or shared 17 Southwestern Athletic Conference championships since joining the league in 1959 and nine national black college championships, including the 1992 title after leading his Tigers to a 10-2 record and a Heritage Bowl victory.

Robinson broke Paul (Bear) Bryant's record for most college wins in 1985. His overall record stood at 405-156-15 at the end of the 1996 campaign.

MARQUIS GRISSOM

If you're a football or basketball player from the Mid-Eastern Athletic Conference, every now and then you receive a little publicity. But if you're a baseball player like Marquis Grissom of Florida A&M, you played in relative obscurity.

Grissom had a great career for the Rattlers. In 1988, he led Florida A&M to the MEAC championship. Playing under Rattlers head coach Robert Lucas, Grissom was named Player of the Year in the MEAC and named to the All-MEAC tournament team.

Grissom, a 5-foot-11, 190-pounder, was a terrific all-around player for the Rattlers. He pitched as well as played in the outfield for FAMU, and in his senior year was 9-3 pitching with a 2.40 ERA. At the plate he hit for a .488

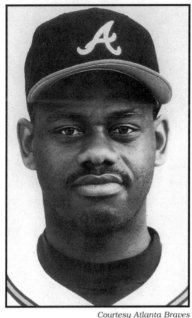

Courtesy Atlanta Braves

Marquis Grissom

average with 12 home runs. He also finished sixth in the NCAA Division I batting race, 38 points ahead of future Houston Astros hitting star Jeff Bagwell.

In 1988, the Montreal Expos selected Grissom in the third round of the free agent draft. In his first season as a professional, Grissom batted .323 with 39 RBIs and 23 stolen bases for Jamestown, Montreal's team in the New York-Pennsylvania League.

The speedy outfielder batted .299 and .278 the next two years for Jacksonville and Indianapolis, prior to being called up to the Expos at the end of the '89 season.

Grissom spent part of the 1990 season on the disabled list. Although he played in only 98 games, he hit .257 while driving in 29 runs and stealing 22 bases.

Over the next two seasons, Grissom gradually developed into one of the best outfielders in the game with his outstanding range.

After leading Florida A&M to a conference championship, Marquis Grissom became a major-leaguer with Montreal and later Atlanta. (Photo courtesy Atlanta Braves)

In fact, he won two Gold Gloves as a center fielder (1993 and 95) and led the league in stolen bases with 76 and 78 in 1991 and 1992.

Although Grissom had played extremely well for Montreal, the Expos traded him in 1995 to the Atlanta Braves for outfielder Roberto Kelly, outfielder Tony Tarasco and pitcher Esteban Yan.

Grissom teamed up with David Justice, Fred McGriff, Tom Glavine and Greg Maddux to help Atlanta defeat the Cleveland Indians in the 1995 World Series.

In addition to winning the World Series, Grissom has appeared in the Major League Baseball All-Star Game in 1993 and 1994.

DOUG WILLIAMS

Doug Williams had the greatest day of his pro career when he led the Washington Redskins in 1987 to a 42-10 romp over the Denver Broncos in Super Bowl XXII. In the process, Williams, a former Grambling star, set four Super Bowl records — most yards passing in a game (340), most yards passing in a quarter (228), most touchdown passes (four) and longest completion (80 yards).

"I had a pretty good pro career," Williams said. "Obviously, winning the Super Bowl with Washington was a big part of my career. I know a lot of people will remember my game in the Super Bowl.

"But I think playing for coach Eddie Robinson really paved the way for me. I mean, coach

Robinson is the most knowledgeable football coach in the country. He taught me a lot about the game and life, too. So I'm glad I had the opportunity to go to Grambling."

A first-team All-American in 1977, Williams finished fourth in the Heisman Trophy voting. He was named MVP

Courtesy Washington Redskins, ©NFL Photos

Doug Williams

of the East-West Shrine Game. Grambling had a 35-5 record during the years that Williams was a starter. During his college career he passed for 8,411 yards and 93 touchdowns.

"I realize the black colleges aren't getting the top high school football players, but I still think they do a great job of developing young athletes," Williams said.

In 1978 he was a first-round draft pick of the Tampa Bay Buccaneers, and he became the first black quarterback to have a major impact in pro football. He was a Buc from 1978-82, starting 33 of that team's first 36 NFL victories, and led them to the playoffs in 1979 and 1981.

Williams spent two years in the United States Football League, playing for the Oklahoma Outlaws and the Arizona Outlaws, respectively. In 1986, he was signed as a free agent and spent two seasons with Washington before retiring from professional football.

But before his retirement, Williams earned a place in NFL history in what may be the most productive quarter of football in the Super Bowl. Trailing Denver 10-0 after the first quarter, Williams brought the Redskins back into the game with a short pass to Ricky Sanders. Sanders was able to get behind the defense and run 80 yards for a touchdown.

It was the beginning of an incredible 15 minutes of play by Washington that resulted in three more touchdown passes of 27, 50 and 8 yards. Williams was nine-for-11 in the quarter for 228 yards. After trailing 10-0 at the beginning of the period, Washington, behind Williams' play, led 35-10 at halftime and went on to win 42-10.

In 1990, he worked for the Black Entertainment Television network doing broadcasts of black college games with Charlie Neal and Lem Barney, and in 1991 he was the athletic director and head coach at Pointe Coupee High School in New Rhoads, La.

"I think coaching in black college football is underrated," Williams said. "I know I was impressed with the coaching and the level of play during the time I did some color work on BET.

"I had a chance to go around the country watching black college football. Black colleges are still turning out great players thanks to a lot of support and good coaching."

Williams worked for the Partnership for a Drug Free Louisiana in 1992, and the following year he became head coach of Northeast High School in Zachary, La. In 1993, he led the school to a 13-1 record and the state semifinals.

In 1994, former Navy head coach George Chaump hired Williams as a running backs coach. He spent two seasons with the Midshipmen. He is currently a scout with the Jacksonville Jaguars.

Rick Mahorn

When Rick Mahorn looks back on his college basketball career at Hampton University, he remembers quick-footed point guard Darryl Warwick, Hank Ford, his college coach, and playing in the Central Intercollegiate Athletic Association.

"Hampton was a great experience for me," said Mahorn, who earned his degree in business administration. "I met a lot of nice people down there. I played with one of the best small-college guards in Darryl Warwick. Darryl played with Gene Banks (former West Philadelphia High, Duke and NBA standout) at West Philadelphia High. He used to penetrate and dish the ball off to me. Thanks to Darryl, I scored a lot of points.

Rick Mahorn, a 6-foot-10-inch forward for the Detroit Pistons played college ball at Hampton University. (Photo courtesy of New Jersey Nets)

"Coach Ford did an excellent job with the basketball program. He and I developed a great relationship. In fact, even today we stay in touch with each other." Ford is now the athletic director at Alfred State University.

"The other thing I remember the most was the CIAA tournament," Mahorn continued. "It's one of the best tournaments in the country. Every year the conference sets a record for attendance."

Mahorn, a three-time National Association for Intercollegiate Athletics (NAIA) All-American, has been a winner throughout his 16-year

NBA career. In 1980, he was drafted by the Washington Bullets in the second round and played five years with the Bullets, leading them to three playoff appearances.

Johnny Most, former Boston Celtics play-by-play man, labeled Mahorn and Jeff Ruland "McFilthy and McNasty," when neither was Irish. Mahorn and Ruland were noted for their physical play around the basket and for their wide-body picks.

In 1985, Mahorn was traded by Washington to Detroit, where his defense and rebounding were key factors in several playoff performances. In 1989, he teamed up with Bill Laimbeer, Dennis Rodman and John Salley to form the "Bad Boys" as the Pistons captured the NBA championship. After the '89 season, Detroit left him unprotected and the Minnesota Timberwolves selected him in the NBA expansion draft.

He didn't spend a lot of time with Minnesota as the Philadelphia 76ers acquired Mahorn in exchange for a first-round pick and two second-round picks in 1991 and 1992. He averaged 10.8 points and 7.6 rebounds a game while helping the 76ers take the Atlantic Division title in 1990.

He and Charles Barkley formed a "Thump and Bump" duo. There were very few players who drove down the middle of the lane with

Mahorn and Barkley inside. Their physical presence was usually felt by the opposing players.

After the 1991 season, the Sixers decided not to re-sign Mahorn, a free agent. So, he signed a contract to play in Italy for a year.

In 1992, Mahorn returned to the United States after signing a contract with the New Jersey Nets. But after four season with the Nets as a backup center and power forward, Mahorn is now back with the Pistons.

STEVE McNAIR

It's not too often that a black college foot-ball player makes the cover of *Sports Illustrated*, finishes third in the Heisman Trophy voting and becomes the third pick in the 1995 NFL draft. But that's what happened to Alcorn State's Steve McNair, who now plays quarterback for the Houston Oilers.

McNair, a 6-foot-2, 224-pounder, was one of the top quarterbacks in college football. He is the only player in NCAA history to gain more than 16,000 yards (16,823) in total offense during his career. The previous high was 14,706 by Ty Detmer of Brigham Young University. McNair set a collegiate record by averaging 400.55 yards in total offense per game (former best: 352.2 by Willie Totten of Mississippi Valley State).

Steve McNair was recruited by a number of major Division I colleges, but his desire to play quarterback led him to Alcorn State. (Photo ©Houston Oilers)

He became only the third player in Division I-AA to throw for 100 touchdowns in a career (119). McNair set an overall NCAA record with an average of 8.18 yards gained per pass play, topping Doug Williams' mark of 7.64. In 1994, he was a unanimous choice for All-American. He completed 928 of 1,673 passes (55.5 percent) for 14,496 yards in passing with 119 TDs and 58 interceptions.

McNair won the Walter Payton Award (top Division I-AA player) and the Eddie Robinson Trophy (top player in black college football). Robinson, Grambling head coach, believes McNair is one of the greatest players to ever play not only in the Southwestern Athletic Conference, but in college football.

The Houston Oilers made Alcorn State quarterback Steve McNair the No. 3 pick in the 1995 NFL draft. (Photo ©Houston Oilers)

"I'm not surprised the Oilers took him in the first round," Robinson said. "He's going to be a great quarterback in the NFL. And believe me, I've seen a lot of quarterbacks. Just here at Grambling we've had James Harris, Doug Williams, Matthew Reed and others. Steve did everything that they did and more. He also did a lot for black college football and the SWAC."

McNair, a native of Mount Olive, Miss., was recruited by a number of major Division I colleges such as Miami, LSU and Mississippi State. But he had no intentions of playing any position except quarterback. So, when Alcorn State moved into the recruiting picture, the decision was very easy. He immediately became the Braves' starting quarterback.

"I could have gone to several major colleges to play football," said McNair, whose older brother, Fred, also played quarterback for the Braves. "It's just that all the Division I schools didn't want me to play quarterback. I wanted to go where I could play right away. Alcorn gave me a chance to play right away."

McNair spent most of his first NFL season as the backup to Houston's No. 1 quarterback, Chris Chandler. As a rookie, he showed some flashes of brilliance when he played the second half of Houston's 24-17 loss to Detroit. In that game, he connected on 16 of 27 passes for 203 yards, one touchdown and one interception.

AL ATTLES

Earl Monroe, Sam Jones and Bobby Dandridge are known for lighting up the CIAA with their offensive talents. But Al Attles, former North Carolina A&T backcourt standout, was a magnificent defensive player.

Attles was known for his long arms and his quick hands. He had the ability to reach around his man and easily take the ball away from him.

"I had a great time playing at North Carolina A&T," Attles said. "We played an exciting brand of basketball.

"I think playing in the CIAA was a wonderful experience for me. The conference has a tremendous following by the fans, students and the alumni."

North Carolina A&T graduate Al Attles starred for the Philadelphia Warriors and later coached the Golden State Warriors. He is now vice president and assistant general manager for the team. (Both photos courtesy Golden State Warriors)

The Aggies' 6-foot-2-inch guard used to steal the ball on a regular basis and glide down to the other end of the court for a layup. People who followed black college basketball in the late '50s will tell you Attles was one of the best defensive players in the CIAA.

Al Attles

"The CIAA had a lot of great players during the time we were at North Carolina A&T," Vince Miller, Attles' college teammate, said. "I mean, guys like Joe Howell (North Carolina A&T) and Cleo Hill (Winston-Salem) could really play. It's just that we didn't receive a lot of publicity at that time.

"But I told everybody how well Al could play and he didn't let me down either. He had a good career in the NBA."

In 1960, Attles was a fifth-round pick of the Philadelphia Warriors. Attles was recommended to the Warriors by his former teammate after Wilt Chamberlain was instrumental in getting the Warriors to hire Miller as a scout. Obviously, Miller made a great recommendation.

"Al was a great player at North Carolina A&T," recalled teammate Vince Miller. "And you know what? Nobody knew anything about him. I recommended Al to Eddie Gottlieb (former owner of the Philadelphia Warriors). Al made the Warriors team and that got me my first scouting job."

During Attles' first 11 seasons, he averaged 8.9 points, 3.5 rebounds and 3.5 assists. His statistics do not represent the physical style of play that earned him the nickname, "The Destroyer."

Attles' biggest moment as a player came on March 2, 1962, in a game against the New York Knicks in Hershey, Pa. He teamed up with Wilt Chamberlain to score 117 points, the most points ever scored by a pair of players in a single game. That was the night Chamberlain scored 100 points himself. Nevertheless, Attles has a spot in the NBA record books along with the league's greatest player.

As a head coach, Attles compiled a 555-516 (.518) record making him the 14th winningest coach in NBA history. He capped off a 48-34 regular-season campaign in the 1974-75 season by guiding the Warriors to the NBA championship with a 4-0 sweep of the Washington Bullets. That Warriors team was led by Rick Barry, Keith Wilkes, Clifford Ray, George Johnson, Derrick Dickey, Phil Smith, Charles Dudley and Charles Johnson.

The next season he led the team to a franchise-best 59-23 record. Attles was named to coach the Western Conference All-Star teams for both the 1975 and 1976 games.

Attles, 59, recently finished his 36th season with the Warriors. His No. 16 jersey which hangs from the Oakland Coliseum rafters brings back memories of his playing days with the Warriors.

Attles, a native of Newark, N.J., now serves as the team's vice president and general manager.

Along with his full-time duties with the Warriors, he also finds the time to regularly visit schools throughout the Bay Area and is a highly sought after motivational speaker. His commitment to the community and his achievements as a player and coach helped him earn an induction into the Bay Area Sports Hall of Fame in 1993. He was also inducted into the New Jersey Sportswriters Hall of Fame in 1991.

The only Golden State head coach to win an NBA championship returned to the bench in 1995 to assist interim head coach Bob Lanier in coaching the final 37 games. In addition, Attles coached in the Rookie All-Star Game in Phoenix that same year.

VIVIAN STRINGER

Vivian Stringer, in a number of ways, is like Temple coach John Chaney. Both Stringer and Chaney were marvelous basketball coaches at Cheyney State College. In fact, they both shared the same gymnasium for practice at Cheyney State. Moreover, they both went on to prove they were not only two of the country's finest small college coaches, but two of the best coaches in college basketball — period.

Stringer spent 12 seasons at Cheyney State compiling an amazing 251-51 record. She led the Lady Wolves to the national championship game in the inaugural NCAA Tournament in 1982. Her top players were All-Americans Yolanda Laney and Val Walker.

Rutgers and former Cheyney State coach Vivian Stringer is a three-time national coach of the year. She has coached teams to 11 appearances in the NCAA Tournament and two trips to the Final Four including a national championship by Cheyney State in 1982. (Photo courtesy Rutgers University)

After a sensational coaching career at Cheyney State, she moved on to the University of Iowa and elevated the Lady Hawkeyes to the top of the Big 10.

She is the winningest coach in Iowa's history with a 269-84 (762.) overall mark in 12 years. She is the only coach to lead the Hawkeyes to ten 20-win seasons, nine NCAA Tournaments, six Big Ten Conference titles and an appearance in the NCAA Final Four. With Iowa's first-ever appearance in the NCAA Final Four in the 1992-93 season, Stringer became the first coach to lead two different schools to the Women's Final Four.

In 1994, she became the third active coach to reach the 500-win plateau with a 78-56 victory over Michigan, and her 533 career victories through the end of the 1995-96 season, make her the third-winningest active coach in Division I women's basketball.

In 1995, Stringer, a native of Edenborn, Pa., and an alumnus of Slippery Rock State College, became the head coach of Rutgers University. Although she struggled in her first season with the Scarlet Knights, Stringer appeared to have the program headed in the right direction. Rutgers' 13-15 record included a 69-67 win over seventh-ranked Penn State and Notre Dame, also ranked among the nation's top women's basketball teams.

Despite a late start, Stringer went right to work on recruiting and signed four All-Americans during the early signing period, and later inked two more players for the 1996-97 season who will comprise a freshman class ranked among the top recruiting classes in the nation.

John Chaney, her former co-worker at Cheyney State, said Rutgers made the right move. Upon learning of Rutgers' decision to make Stringer the head coach of the women's program, Chaney enthusiastically agreed with the move.

"This is the biggest step that Rutgers could ever take in getting, in my opinion, the best woman at what she does," Chaney said.

A three-time National Coach of the Year (1993, 1988 and 1982) and NCAA District V Coach of the Year (1993, 1988 and 1985), Stringer was also honored as the Big Ten Coach of the Year in 1993 and 1991, and was the 1993 recipient of the Carol Eckman Award, given annually to the women's basketball coach who best demonstrates spirit, courage, integrity, commitment, leadership and service to the game of women's basketball.

Jolette Law, former Iowa All-American and current Scarlet Knight assistant coach, is one among many who list Stringer as a positive role model.

Vivian Stringer began her second season at Rutgers with her first full recruiting class, which has been rated by experts as one of the best in the nation. (Photo courtesy Rutgers University, ©Chris Faytok)

"She's (Stringer) been a mentor to me, a mother figure and definitely a friend," Law said. "I can't find a word in the dictionary to describe her. I had the opportunity to display my talents with the Harlem Globetrotters. I know she can bring the talent out of people.

"She's taught me so much about the game, but also about the game of life. I'm forever indebted to her. I told her that whenever she needs me, I'll go to bat for her."

Stringer has a great deal of international coaching experience. In 1991, she led the United States to the bronze medal at the Pan American Games in Havana, Cuba. She coached the U.S. entry to the 1989 World Championship Zone Qualification Tournament in Sao Paulo, Brazil, and the 1985 World University Games team in Kobe, Japan. She coached in Mexico in 1979 and in 1981 was the head coach of the U.S. Select Team that toured China. She also coached in the 1992 National Sports Festival in Indianapolis, Ind.

Stringer was one of the key figures in the development of the Women's Basketball Coaches Association. She currently is a voting board member of the Amateur Basketball Association of the United States and the Nike Coaches Advisory Board. Stringer served as the Big Ten Conference's representative to the NCAA Division I Mideast Basketball Committee from 1987-

90 and was elected to the Women's Sports Foundation Advisory Board.

In 24 years as a college basketball head coach, Stringer has taken 11 teams to the NCAA Tournament, including two trips to the Final Four and four regional finals. Her overall coaching record stood at 533-149 following the 1995 season.

ANDRE DAWSON

Few baseball players better than Andre Dawson have come out of black colleges. Dawson played for Florida A&M, the school that also produced Vince Coleman and Marquis Grissom.

Dawson, a native of Miami, Florida, and a current member of the Florida Marlins, was selected by Montreal in the 11th round of the free agent draft in 1975. He excelled in the minors before coming up to the Expos in 1977.

Dawson was the National League Rookie of the Year. He batted .282 with 15 home runs and drove in 65 runs while stealing 21 bases.

Dawson, a brilliant right fielder, could run down fly balls to the warning track of most stadiums. He also possessed a strong throwing arm which kept a lot of runners from taking the extra base.

In 1981, he hit .302 with 24 home runs, 64 RBIs and 26 stolen bases, which was good enough to land him a spot on the National League All-Star Team. He led the Expos to a playoff series victory over the Philadelphia Phillies, but Montreal narrowly lost to the Los Angeles Dodgers in the National League Championship Series.

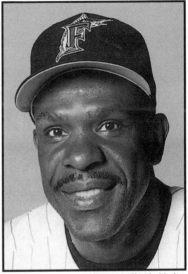

Courtesy Florida Marlins

Andre Dawson

Dawson spent nine years with the Expos before signing a free agent contract with the Chicago Cubs in 1986. This was a great move for him. Dawson chose to play for the Cubs because he felt the grass at Wrigley Field would help to preserve his chronically bad knees. The Cubs didn't believe they could afford him, so he offered to sign a contract and let them fill in the numbers.

The move also paid big dividends for the Cubs. In 1987, Dawson hit a career-high 49 home runs and drove in 137 runs while capturing National League MVP honors and also earning a new contract. During his five seasons with the Cubs, he hit 174 home runs and drove in 587 runs.

In 1992, he signed a free agent contract with the Boston Red Sox, who were hoping to cash in on some of his power. However, Dawson spent most of the next two seasons on the disabled list. Following the '94 season, he was signed by the Marlins and returned to his hometown of Miami. During the 1996 season, he announced that he would retire at the end of the year.

Dawson, an eight-time all-star, has received numerous honors in his career. He was named outfielder on *The Sporting News* National League Silver Slugging team (1980-81, 1983 and 1987). He won the National League Gold Glove as an outfielder (1980-85 and 1987-88).

Dawson has played 20 years of major-league baseball, 18 of them in the National League.

The Central Intercollegiate Athletic Association

Bowie State College .... Bowie, Md.

Elizabeth City State University .... Elizabeth City, N.C.

Norfolk State University .... Norfolk, Va.

Saint Paul's College............................ Lawrenceville, Va.

Virginia State College .... Petersburg, Va.

Virginia Union University.......................... Richmond, Va.

Fayetteville State University .... Fayetteville, N.C.

Johnson C. Smith University .... Charlotte, N.C.

Livingstone College .... Salisbury, N.C.

North Carolina Central University .... Durham, N.C.

Saint Augustine's College .... Raleigh, N.C.

Shaw University .... Raleigh, N.C.

Winston-Salem State University....... Winston-Salem, N.C.

Hampton University .... Hampton, Va.

The Central Intercollegiate Athletic Association (CIAA) was founded in 1912 as the Colored Intercollegiate Athletic Association. Having been in existence for more than 80 years, the CIAA is the oldest black athletic conference in the nation. Although the membership has changed since 1912, all CIAA member institutions are Historically Black Colleges and Universities (HBCUs), spanning the East Coast from Maryland to North Carolina.

Many institutions currently in the Mid-Eastern Athletic Conference (MEAC) were once affiliated with the CIAA. The CIAA is headquartered in Hampton, Va., and is governed by a board of directors comprised of 13 presidents/chancellors of the member schools.

The CIAA is one of the largest Division II Conferences in the National Collegiate Athletic Association (NCAA) and is at the forefront of Division II in terms of exposure to fans and media.

The CIAA annually holds the third-largest basketball tournament in the country in terms of attendance, ranking only behind the Atlantic Coast Conference (ACC) and Big East tourna-

Virginia Union University is located in Richmond, Va. (Photo courtesy of Virginia Union University)

ments. The CIAA has also developed an aggressive television package which is currently syndicated over a combination of local, regional and cable networks across the country.

The CIAA represents the embodiment of quality athletics. The conference holds championships annually in cross country, volleyball, football, men's and women's basketball, men's and women's indoor and outdoor track and field, tennis, golf, baseball and softball.

In 1989, the CIAA claimed five national championship titles: men's indoor and outdoor track (Saint Augustine's College), tennis (Hampton University), men's basketball (North Carolina Central University) and golf (Livingstone College). Virginia Union University was the Division II men's national champion in basketball in 1980 and 1992. The women's national championship has been held by both Hampton University (1988) and Virginia Union (1983).

Saint Augustine's College captured both the indoor and outdoor men's track and field championship titles in 1995 and has held the outdoor track title seven years in a row and the indoor track title four times since 1990. Saint Augustine's head track and field coach George Williams served as a coach on the USA Track Team and assisted in the 1996 Olympics in Atlanta.

The CIAA regularly sends several teams into the NCAA Division II playoffs in basketball. In each year since 1991 at least three men's basketball teams have participated in postseason play. The dominance of CIAA members in Division II basketball was evidenced after the 1995 season when all four teams participating in the NCAA regional playoffs in Fayetteville, N.C., were CIAA schools (Johnson C. Smith University, Norfolk State University, Shaw University and Virginia Union University). Norfolk State

Hampton University students can get hands-on training in all aspects of the broadcast media. (Photo courtesy Hampton University)

University advanced to the Division II semifinals and Corey Williams of the Spartans was named Division II Player of the Year.

Under the leadership of coach James Sweat, the Norfolk State Spartanettes have participated in postseason play each year since 1990. Two-time Kodak All-American Kristie Greene and NCAA Division II assist leader Lisa Rice both finished their college careers in 1995 under the leadership of Sweat. Dave Robbins, Virginia Union head basketball coach, is the winningest active coach in NCAA Division II, while Sweat is ranked in the top five for women's coaches.

CIAA athletes have also experienced success after college. Charles Oakley (Virginia Union, New York Knicks), Rick Mahorn (Hampton, New Jersey Nets), Darrell Armstrong (Fayetteville, Orlando Magic) and Terry Davis (Virginia Union, Dallas Mavericks) all currently represent the CIAA in the NBA. Past NBA greats include Bobby Dandridge (Norfolk State), Al Attles (North Carolina A&T), Earl Monroe (Winston-Salem State University) and Sam Jones (North Carolina Central University). John McLendon and Clarence "Big House" Gaines represent great basketball coaching alumni from the CIAA schools.

Football players like Yancy Thigpen (Winston-Salem, Pittsburgh Steelers), Ben Coates (Livingstone, New England Patriots), Bobby Phillips (Virginia Union, Minnesota Vikings), Robert Massey (North Carolina Central, Detroit Lions), Anthony Blaylock (Winston-Salem, Chicago Bears) and James Brown (Virginia State, New York Jets) have appeared on the NFL gridiron.

The premiere event in the CIAA is the annual CIAA basketball tournament. The first tournament was held in 1946, and celebrated its 50th anniversary in 1995. The tournament has grown from a 2,000-person sellout in Washington, D.C., to a capacity crowd at its current home in Winston-Salem, N.C. The tournament has visited the North Carolina cities of Winston-Salem, Greensboro and Durham, and the Virginia cities of Hampton, Norfolk and Richmond.

Recently, the CIAA Board of Directors awarded the 1997-99 tournament bid to Winston-Salem. The tournament consists of an entire week of basketball action, including all 13 women's and men's teams participating in a single elimination format. The week culminates in championship games on Saturday for both the men's and women's teams.

CIAA Tournament Week has become more than just a basketball tournament. Many social and alumni functions are held during the week, including recognition of past and present athletes at Tip Off Banquets and CIAA Hall of Fame inductions. The cheerleaders, pep bands and "Old Timers" all play a part in CIAA excitement. The goal of the CIAA is not only to produce the best basketball in the country, but to give the fans a week of fun they will never forget.

Current estimates by host city officials reveal that tournament fans generate approximately $8 million in revenue for their city during the week of the tournament. Hotels are typically filled to capacity, with retail establishments selling out of food and apparel. Newspaper and television coverage are abundant during tournament week.

The CIAA encourages minority participation in the tournament wherever possible, and has offered vending opportunities at the tournament site for small business entrepreneurs. Additional opportunities exist for sponsorship of other tournament events associated with the tournament or by advertisement in the souvenir program.

The CIAA is entering the second half century of its basketball heritage. As the CIAA continues to change and grow, we are confident that the legend of the CIAA will continue.

Mid-Eastern Athletic Conference

Coppin State College .... Baltimore, Md.

Delaware State University .... Dover, Del.

Howard University .... Washington, D.C.

University of Md. Eastern Shore .... Princess Anne, Md.

Morgan State University .... Baltimore, Md.

N. Carolina A&T State University .... Greensboro, N.C.

South Carolina State University .... Orangeburg, S.C.

Bethune-Cookman College .... Daytona Beach, Fla.

Florida A&M University .... Tallahassee, Fla.

In 1969, a bold ad hoc group of innovators long associated with intercollegiate athletics, met to discuss the feasibility of organizing a new conference based along the Atlantic coast. Dissected from these meetings, a steering and planning committee was formed to fully investigate the idea, present a detailed report with recommendations to interested collegiate institutions, then construct a workshop to outline proposals.

A number of representatives from neophyte institutions later convened to listen to the committee's report, which led to a two-day scrutinized discussion about the proposed organization and its procedures. After adopting the program, seven of the institutions agreed to become the Mid-Eastern Athletic Conference (MEAC).

In 1970, the league was confirmed with these seven institutions: Delaware State University, Howard University, University of Maryland Eastern Shore, Morgan State University, North Carolina A&T University, North Carolina Central University and South Carolina State College.

In 1978, a milestone was reached when the MEAC selected Kenneth A. Free to be its first full-time commissioner. Free held this position

Belcher Hall houses the School of Business at South Carolina State University (above) in Orangeburg, S.C., while football games are played in Oliver C. Dawson Bulldog Stadium (below). Originally constructed in 1955 to seat 8,000, the facility was later renovated and enlarged and now seats 22,000 fans. (Photo and illustration courtesy South Carolina State University)

for 18 years before leaving the conference to go into private business. Charles Harris has succeeded him as the new commissioner.

Free had been preceded by three interim commissioners: Dr. Leroy Walker (1971-74, currently president of the United States Olympic Committee), Earl Mason (1974-75) and Dr. James Younge (1975-78). Original members Morgan State, NCCU and UMES withdrew from the conference at the close of the 1979 fiscal year. However, UMES was readmitted in 1981 and Morgan in 1984. Florida A&M opted to resign in 1984, but was readmitted in 1986. Coppin State College was granted admittance in 1985, and the MEAC's 10th member, Hampton University, was admitted in 1995.

Historical progress continued when the MEAC satisfied necessary NCAA criteria to be classified as a Division I conference on June 8, 1980, and just a month later, was granted an automatic berth to participate in the NCAA Division I basketball championships. The MEAC also qualified for automatic entry in the NCAA Division I-AA football championships in 1981, 1982 and 1986. At-large entries were extended in 1992 and 1993. Howard completed the 1993 regular season undefeated, becoming the only MEAC team to accomplish that feat.

The MEAC has achieved a number of accomplishments in intercollegiate athletics. In

The Delaware State University band gets ready for another performance on the same football field where NFL star John Taylor played during his college days. (Photo courtesy Delaware State University)

football, South Carolina State won the MEAC titles in 1981 and 1982 for the seventh and eighth times and reached the second round of the I-AA championship both years. Morgan grabbed the 1979 crown and represented the MEAC in the Division II championships. In addition to the NCAA postseason play, MEAC teams have appeared in nine NCAA-sanctioned bowl games and two Orange Blossom Classics.

The National Football League, Canadian Football League and World Football League sparkle with many MEAC players. Plus, former Bethune-Cookman coach Larry Little was named coach of the WFL's Ohio Glory in 1992. The

MEAC was also instrumental in constructing the Freedom Bowl All-Star Classic and the Heritage Bowl. Participants have been North Carolina A&T (1991), and South Carolina State (1993, 1994).

In basketball, Howard University won the 1981 MEAC tournament and became the first MEAC team to play in the NCAA Division I basketball championships. MEAC runner-up, North Carolina A&T, was then invited to play in the 1981 National Invitation Tournament. In 1982, North Carolina A&T started a string of seven consecutive NCAA appearances.

The 1981 NIT trip was North Carolina A&T's second, having participated in 1976. However, UMES had preceded the Aggies by reaching the NIT second round in 1974. But Morgan State made the biggest splash during the professional league's draft process. In 1991, the MEAC matched its 1981 feat by having two different teams in a national championship series, FAMU in the NCAA and Coppin State in the NIT. The league repeated this accomplishment in 1995 as North Carolina A&T went to the NCAA Tournament and Coppin State participated in the NIT.

In women's basketball, South Carolina State won the AIAW national championship in 1979. Howard became the first MEAC women's team to participate in an NCAA Division I champion-

The School of Technology at North Carolina A&T University is the No. 1 producer of minoirty students in industrial technology and is among the top producers of technology students in the country. (Photo courtesy North Carolina A&T University)

ship after winning the 1982 conference tournament. South Carolina State followed in 1983 with a first-round victory, and holds the distinction as the only MEAC team, men's or women's, to have a win in this event.

In soccer, Howard University miraculously won the 1974 NCAA Division I championship. The Bison were selected to play in the NCAA playoffs seven times since 1971, and reached the championship game in 1988.

Outdoor track and field has always been a competitive MEAC sport, and NCCU won the first three conference titles and finished fourth in the 1974 NCAA Division I finals. One of the NCAA stars, Larry Black, was a member of the 1972 Olympic 400-meter relay team that won the gold medal, and he later won the silver in the 200-meter dash.

MEAC women began league competition in 1980. South Carolina State's women won the 1982 national AIAW Division II championship.

The MEAC initiated cross country in 1980 and indoor track in 1981. Tennis and golf returned as MEAC-governed sports in 1981 after a five-year hiatus. Golf was later discontinued after the 1982 championship, but kingpin South Carolina State has continued its excellence with National Minority College championships in 1987 and 1988.

Women's volleyball was added as an MEAC-governed sport in 1983. That same year, baseball which had been discontinued following the 1977 season, was again added, while women's softball was added in 1992. In baseball, the MEAC was granted an entry into the 1994 NCAA championship play-in-format, and FAMU earned the honor as the MEAC team to participate.

In wrestling, Morgan State has won 13 of 23 championships and the MEAC individual championships were granted automatic entry into the 1986 NCAA championships. Despite the loss of an automatic bid, many MEAC wrestlers have been invited as at-large participants. The MEAC gained a softball play-in-position in 1995, and FAMU became the first MEAC representative.

SOUTHERN INTERCOLLEGIATE ATHLETIC CONFERENCE

Setting the Standard in Intercollegiate Athletics for Over 80 Years

Alabama A&M University .... Normal, Ala.

Albany State College .... Albany, Ga.

Clark Atlanta University .... Atlanta, Ga.

Fort Valley State College .... Fort Valley, Ga.

Kentucky State University .... Frankfort, Ky.

LeMoyne-Owen College .... Memphis, Tenn.

Miles College .... Birmingham, Ala.

Morehouse College .... Atlanta, Ga.

Morris Brown College .... Atlanta, Ga.

Paine College .... Augusta, Ga.

Savannah State College .... Savannah, Ga.

Tuskegee University .... Tuskegee, Ala.

The Southern Intercollegiate Athletic Conference (SIAC) was founded in 1913, and today, more than 80 years later, the conference is still one of the most viable forces in athletics among the nation's collegiate systems.

On Dec. 30, 1913, representatives of the following institutions met at Morehouse College to consider the regulations of intercollegiate athletics among black colleges in the Southeast: Alabama State University, Atlanta University, Clark College, Morehouse College, Morris Brown College, Talladega College and Tuskegee Institute.

The representatives formed a permanent organization, the Southeastern Intercollegiate Athletic Conference, which has had a continuous history ever since. In 1929, the name was changed to the Southern Intercollegiate Athletic Conference.

Three institutions have held continuous membership in the conference: Clark College (now Clark Atlanta University), Morris Brown College and Tuskegee University.

Other institutions which have held membership are Allen University, Benedict College,

Bethune-Cookman College, Edward Waters College, Fisk University, Florida A&M University, Jackson State University, Knoxville College, Lane College, Rust College, South Carolina State University, Stillman College, Tennessee State University and Xavier University.

The present membership is composed of 12 different institutions in four states (Alabama, Georgia, Kentucky and Tennessee): Alabama A&M University, Albany State College, Clark Atlanta University, Fort Valley State College, Kentucky State University, LeMoyne-Owen College, Miles College, Morehouse College, Morris Brown College, Paine College, Savannah State College and Tuskegee University.

The SIAC is a member of the National Collegiate Athletic Association (NCAA) and participates at the Division II level, annually sponsoring six men's (cross country, football, basketball, tennis, outdoor track and field, and baseball) and five women's championships (cross country, volleyball, basketball, tennis, and outdoor track and field).

SIAC teams and its athletes are known for being staunch competitors and for excelling on the national level. The conference as a whole has claimed more than 50 team and individual national championships.

In 1978, Florida A&M became the first black college to win the NCAA Division I-AA national

A monument to Booker T. Washington, founder of Tuskegee University stands at the entrance of the school. (Photo courtesy Tuskegee University)

football championship when it defeated Massachusetts 35-28 in the finals. The SIAC also has more than 300 former and current professional football players.

Some of the retired NFL players that played in the SIAC are: NFL Hall of Famer John Stallworth of Alabama A&M, Larry Little and Jack McClarien of Bethune-Cookman, Rayfield Wright of Fort Valley State, Bob Hayes of Florida A&M, Alfred Jenkins, Tommy Hart and Ezra Johnson of Morris Brown, John Gilliam of South Carolina State, Oliver Ross of Alabama A&M and Deacon Jones.

The current professional players include All-Pros Greg Lloyd of the Pittsburgh Steelers (Fort Valley State) and Shannon Sharpe of the Denver Broncos (Savannah State), as well as Anthony Abrams of the Washington Redskins (Clark Atlanta), Eddie Anderson of the Los Angeles Raiders (Albany State), Howard Ballard of the Seattle Seahawks (Alabama A&M), Charles Evans of the Minnesota Vikings (Clark Atlanta), Dan Land of the Los Angeles Raiders (Albany State), Fred Lester of the New York Jets (Alabama A&M), Joe Patton of the Washington Redskins (Alabama A&M) and Barry Wagner of the Indianapolis Colts (Alabama A&M).

The SIAC is also home to football coaching legends Alonzo Smith (Jake) Gaither and Cleveland Leigh (Major) Abbott.

Dr. Martin Luther King Jr., Edwin Moses and Spike Lee are among many distinguished alumni of Morehouse College in Atlanta, Ga. (Photo courtesy Morehouse College)

Gaither, a member of the National Football Foundation Hall of Fame, won 203 football games while losing 36, and he tied four. He guided Florida A&M to six black college national championships and his Rattlers won the SIAC championship 22 of 25 years he coached college football.

Tuskegee University is the only college or university in the United States to be designated a unit of the National Park Service and a National Historic Site. Among the many well-known buildings on the 4,500-acre campus is Tomkins Hall, above. (Photo courtesy Tuskegee University)

Cleve Abbott coached all sports at Tuskegee in 1923, and he served there continuously from 1923 to 1955. He won 11 SIAC football championships and seven black college national championships. Abbott had a total of six undefeated seasons, and the Tigers went 46 consecutive games without a loss in the mid-1920s. From 1936-56, Abbott's women's track and field teams at Tuskegee participated in 36 national AAU championships and won 25.

Two of the first four blacks selected to play in the NBA were from the SIAC. Some of the former stars who have enjoyed success in the NBA include the Jones brothers — Caldwell, Charles, Major and Wilbert of Albany State; Clemon Johnson of Florida A&M; and Harold Ellis of Morehouse College.

On the coaching side, John Chaney and the late Ed Adams have ties to the SIAC. Adams coached at Tuskegee and during his 23-year span won 645 games and only lost 153 for an .811 winning percentage. He was a member of the 1934 Tuskegee team that won the first SIAC basketball tournament championship, and he was the first black basketball coach to win 500 games. Chaney is currently coaching at Temple University. He also was one of the SIAC's outstanding players in the 1950s while at Bethune-Cookman.

The first black female to win a gold medal in any Olympic sport, Alice Coachman Davis, came from the SIAC. Coachman Davis won an Olympic gold medal in the high jump at the 1948 Olympic Games in London with a jump of 5 feet, $6^{1}/_{8}$ inches. She also won the AAU high jump title for 10 consecutive years.

Other SIAC Olympic Gold Medalists include Catherine Hardy of Fort Valley State (400-meter relay in 1952); Mildred McDaniel of Tuskegee (high jump in 1956); Bob Hayes of Florida A&M (100-meter dash in 1964); Edwin Moses of Morehouse College (400-meter hurdles in 1976 and 1984) and went 10 years without a loss in

Savannah State College in Savannah, Ga., was chartered in 1890 by the state of Georgia. (Photo courtesy Savannah State College)

hurdle competition; and Dannette Young (400-meter relay in 1988).

The SIAC has also had two Olympic coaches including Barbara Jacket (a graduate of Tuskegee University) at the 1992 games.

Another SIAC track and field standout is Evelyn Lawler. She is a graduate of Tuskegee University and won a gold medal at the Pan American Games. Lawler is the mother of Olympic gold medalist Carl Lewis.

In 1957, Althea Gibson of Florida A&M became the first black to win the singles title at Wimbledon, and she is a member of the National Lawn Tennis Hall of Fame.

The SIAC also has had its share of success in major league baseball, which includes a World Series MVP. Don Clendenon of Morehouse College was the MVP of the 1969 World Series when he played with the New York Mets. Cleon Jones of Alabama A&M also played with the Mets, while Andre Dawson of the Florida Marlins played at Florida A&M, and Vince Coleman, who has played with St. Louis, Kansas City and Cincinnati, played at Florida A&M.

Former Florida A&M players retired from baseball, but who had successful careers in the majors, are Greg Coleman and Bill Lucas. After concluding his major-league baseball career, Lucas became the first black general manager in baseball when the Atlanta Braves appointed him to that position.

A banner year for the SIAC was 1993 when member institutions competed for NCAA Division II championships in eight different sports. In football, Albany State went 11-0 during the regular season and made its first trip to the playoffs; Alabama A&M's men and women competed in the Indoor Track and Field championships and both finished in the top five.

In men's basketball, Alabama A&M participated in the playoffs and in women's basketball Fort Valley State made its second straight trip to the playoffs. Alabama A&M's men's cross country team won the Southeastern Regional title and finished eighth at the nationals. At the Outdoor Track and Field championships, Alabama A&M's men finished 10th and the women claimed their second consecutive national title.

The SIAC is also home of the longest running rivalry in black college football, and to the winningest team in black college football. Morehouse and Tuskegee have been doing battle since 1904. Tuskegee celebrated its 102nd season in 1996, and during the past century has amassed 490 victories — first among historically black colleges and universities.

All SIAC member institutions have a rich athletic history. They rely heavily on past leadership to help them face today's challenges as they continue their quests to excel in collegiate athletics. Collectively, these institutions provide an excellent portrayal of the conference slogan — *The Magnificent Twelve.*

Southwestern

Athletic Conference

Alabama State University .... Montgomery, Ala.

Alcorn State University .... Lorman, Miss.

Grambling State University .... Grambling, La.

Jackson State University .... Jackson, Miss.

Mississippi Valley State University .... Itta Bena, Miss.

Prairie View A&M University .... Prairie View, Texas

Southern University .... Baton Rouge, La.

Texas Southern University .... Houston, Texas

The Southwestern Athletic Conference was founded in 1920 and had an original membership of six colleges. The original "Super Six" consisted of Bishop College, Paul Quinn College, Sam Houston College, Prairie View College, Texas College and Wiley College. Its founding fathers were C.H. Fuller of Bishop College, E.G. Evans, H.J. Evans, H.J. Mason and Willie Stams of Prairie View; Red Randolph and C.H. Patterson of Paul Quinn; G. Whitte Jordan of Wiley; and D.C. Fuller of Texas College.

Paul Quinn became the first of the original SWAC members to withdraw from the league in 1929. When Langston University of Oklahoma was admitted into the conference two years later, it began the migration of state-supported institutions into the SWAC. Southern University of Baton Rouge, La., entered the ranks in 1934, followed by Arkansas AM&N of Pine Bluff, Ark., in 1936 and Texas Southern University of Houston, Texas, in 1954.

Rapid growth in enrollment of the state-supported schools made it difficult for the church-supported schools to finance their athletic pro-

Jack Spinks Stadium, opened in 1992, seats 20,000 for football games at Alcorn State. The facility was named for former star running back Jack Spinks, who was the first Alcorn player and first black in Mississippi to play professional football. (Illustration courtesy of Alcorn State University)

grams and one-by-one they fell victim to the growing prowess of the tax-supported colleges.

Bishop College withdrew from the conference in 1956, Langston in 1957 and Sam Houston in 1959, one year after the admittance of two more state-supported colleges — Grambling College of Grambling, La., and Jackson State of Jackson, Miss.

The enter-exit cycle continued in 1961 when Texas College withdrew, followed by the admittance of Alcorn A&M College of Lorman, Miss., in 1962. Wiley left in 1968, the same year that Mississippi Valley State College of Itta Bena, Miss., entered. Arkansas AM&N exited in 1970 and Alabama State University of Montgomery, Ala., entered the league in 1982.

Today, the SWAC ranks among the nation's elite in terms of alumni playing with professional teams. In football, the SWAC has produced some outstanding NFL players over the years such as Doug Williams, Paul (Tank) Younger, Willie Davis and Willie Brown from Grambling; Walter Payton, Lem Barney and Harold Jackson from Jackson State; Eddie Robinson from Alabama State; Roynell Young and Steve McNair from Alcorn State; Jerry Rice from Mississippi Valley State; and others.

The NBA has seen numerous SWAC alumni such as Larry Smith (Alcorn State), Willis Reed (Grambling), Purvis Short and Lindsey Hunter (Jackson State), and Avery Johnson and Bobby Phills (Southern University).

Its current membership of Alabama State, Alcorn State, Grambling State, Jackson State, Mississippi Valley State, Prairie View A&M, Southern University-Baton Rouge and Texas Southern University are all NCAA Division I members, Division I-AA in football.

Championship competition offered by the SWAC includes title races for men in baseball, basketball, cross country, football, golf, indoor and outdoor track, and tennis. Women's com-

Grambling State University offers students a wide range of educational choices. (Photo courtesy Grambling State University)

petition is offered in the sports of basketball, cross country, golf, indoor and outdoor track, tennis and volleyball.

The conference celebrated its 75th anniversary during the 1995-96 school year.

SHERIDAN BLACK NETWORK
ALL-TIME BLACK COLLEGE
FOOTBALL TEAM

Quarterback .... Doug Williams, Grambling

Running Backs .... Walter Payton, Jackson State
Paul "Tank" Younger, Grambling

Wide Receivers .... Jerry Rice, Mississippi Valley State
John Stallworth, Alabama A&M
Charlie Joiner, Grambling

Offensive Linemen .... Art Shell, Maryland State
Rayfield Wright, Fort Valley State
Jackie Slater, Jackson State
Larry Little, Bethune-Cookman
Ernie Barnes, N. Carolina Central

Defensive Linemen .... Willie Davis, Grambling
Ed "Too Tall" Jones, Tennessee State
David "Deacon" Jones, Mississippi Vocational
L.C. Greenwood, Arkansas AM&N

Linebackers .... Robert Brazille, Jackson State
Harry Carson, South Carolina State
Willie Lanier, Morgan State

Defensive Backs .... Mel Blount, Southern
Lem Barney, Jackson State
Donnie Shell, South Carolina State
Everson Walls, Grambling

Source: *Black College Football 1892-1992*
One Hundred Years of History, Education and Pride
by Michael Hurd, The Donning Company

BLACK COLLEGE PLAYERS IN PRO SPORTS

BLACK COLLEGE
PLAYERS IN THE NFL

Name	Pos.	School	NFL Team
Brent Alexander	DB	Tennessee St.	Arizona
Stevie Anderson	WR	Grambling	Arizona
Marcus Dowdell	WR/KR	Tennessee St.	Arizona
Larry Tharpe	T	Tennessee St.	Arizona
Aeneas Williams	DB	Southern	Arizona
Bernard Wilson	DT	Tennessee St.	Arizona
Richard Huntley	RB	Winston-Salem	Atlanta
Nate Newton	G	Florida A&M	Dallas
Erik Williams	T	Central St.	Dallas
Robert Harris	DE	Southern	New York
Michael Strahan	DE	Texas Southern	New York
Darion Connor	LB	Jackson St.	Philadelphia
Lester Holmes	G	Jackson St.	Philadelphia
Jimmie Johnson	TE	Howard	Philadelphia
Kevin Johnson	DT	Texas Southern	Philadelphia
Michael Samson	DT	Grambling	Philadelphia
Freddie Solomon	WR	S. Carolina St.	Philadelphia
Dexter Nottage	DE	Florida A&M	Washington
Joe Patton	G	Alabama A&M	Washington

Former Jackson State University star Lester Holmes now plays for the Philadelphia Eagles. (Photo by Ed Mahan)

Name	Pos.	School	NFL Team
Michael Hicks	RB	S. Carolina St.	Chicago
John Thierry	DE	Alcorn St.	Chicago
James Williams	T	Cheyney St.	Chicago
Zefross Moss	T	Alabama St.	Detroit
Robert Porcher	DT	S. Carolina St.	Detroit
Kevin Waldroup	DL	Central St.	Detroit
Terry Mickens	WR	Florida A&M	Green Bay
Roderick Mullen	S	Grambling	Green Bay
Roderick Mullen	DB	Grambling	Green Bay
Charles Evans	RB	Clark-Atlanta	Minnesota
Jake Reed	WR	Grambling	Minnesota
Fernando Smith	DE	Jackson St.	Minnesota
Sean Vanhorse	DB	Howard	Minnesota
Jay Walker	QB	Howard	Minnesota
Kenneth Gant	S	Albany St.	Tampa Bay
Brandon Hayes	T	Central St.	Carolina
Brett Maxie	S	Texas Southern	Carolina
Tyrone Poole	CB	Fort Valley St.	Carolina
Torrance Small	WR	Alcorn St.	New Orleans
Donald Willis	G	N. Carolina A&T	New Orleans
Alberto White	DE	Texas Southern	St. Louis
Dwayne White	G	Alcorn St.	St. Louis
Rod Milstead	G	Delaware St.	San Francisco
Jerry Rice	WR	Miss. Valley St.	San Francisco
Marlo Perry	LB	Jackson St.	Buffalo
Emanuel Martin	DB	Alabama St.	Buffalo
Kendel Shello	DT	Southern	Indianapolis
Richard Dent	DE	Tennessee St.	Indianapolis
James Brown	T	Virginia St.	Miami
Ben Coates	TE	Livingstone	New England
Will Moore	WR	Texas Southern	New England
Larry Tharpe	T	Tennessee St.	New England

Both photos courtesy Alcorn State University

Torrance Small
New Orleans Saints
(Alcorn State)

John Thierry
Chicago Bears
(Alcorn State)

Name	Pos.	School	NFL Team
Reggie White	NT	N. Carolina A&T	New England
Devins Wyman	DT	Kentucky St.	New England
Hugh Douglas	DE	Central St.	New York
Everett McIver	G	Elizabeth City	New York
Herman Arvie	G	Grambling	Baltimore
Orlando Brown	OL	S. Carolina St.	Baltimore
Anthony Pleasant	DE	Tennessee St.	Baltimore
James Roe	WR	Norfolk St.	Baltimore
Bennie Thompson	S	Grambling	Baltimore
Wally Williams	C-G	Florida A&M	Baltimore
Ashley Ambrose	DB	Miss. Valley St.	Cincinnati
Roger Jones	DB	Tennessee St.	Cincinnati
Anthony Cook	DE-DT	S. Carolina St.	Houston
Steve McNair	QB	Alcorn St.	Houston
Reggie Barlow	WR	Alabama St.	Jacksonville

Name	Pos.	School	NFL Team
Tony Kimbrough	WR	Jackson St.	Jacksonville
Robert Massey	DB	N. Carolina Central	Jacksonville
Eddie Robinson	LB	Alabama St.	Jacksonville
Jimmy Smith	WR	Jackson St.	Jacksonville
Terence Warren	WR	Hampton	Jacksonville
Greg Lloyd	LB	Fort Valley St.	Pittsburgh
Yancey Thigpen	WR	Winston-Salem St.	Pittsburgh
Shannon Sharpe	TE	Savannah St.	Denver
Jamie Brown	T	Florida A&M	Denver
Tony Stargell	DB	Tennessee St.	Kansas City
Eddie Anderson	S	Fort Valley St.	Oakland
Andrew Glover	TE	Grambling	Oakland
Marcus Hinton	TE	Alcorn St.	Oakland
Dan Land	DB-S	Albany St.	Oakland
Albert Lewis	DB	Grambling	Oakland
Gerald Perry	T	Southern	Oakland
Dwayne Harper	DB	S. Carolina St.	San Diego
Howard Ballard	T	Alabama A&M	Seattle

Bobby Phills of the Cleveland Cavaliers played his college ball at Southern University. (Photo courtesy Cleveland Cavaliers)

BLACK COLLEGE PLAYERS IN THE NBA

Name	Pos.	School	NBA Team
Charles Oakley	F	Virginia Union	New York
Anthony Mason	F	Tennessee St.	Charlotte
Bobby Phills	G	Southern	Cleveland
Marcus Mann	F	Miss. Valley St.	Golden St.
Lindsey Hunter	G	Jackson St.	Detroit

(Detroit Pistons photo)

Lindsey Hunter, Detroit
(Jackson State)

(Toronto Raptors photo)

Carlos Rogers, Toronto
(Tennessee State)

Name	Pos.	School	NBA Team
Emanuel Davis	G	Deleware St.	Houston
Charles Jones	F	Albany St.	Houston
Rick Mahorn	F	Hampton	Detroit
Darrell Armstrong	G	Fayetteville St.	Orlando
Priest Lauderdale	C	Central St.	Atlanta
Avery Johnson	G	Southern	San Antonio
Larry Stewart	F	Coppin St.	Seattle
Carlos Rogers	F	Tennessee St.	Toronto
Ben Wallace	F	Virginia Union	Washington

BLACK COLLEGE PLAYERS IN MLB

Name	Pos.	School	MLB Team
Marquis Grissom	OF	Florida A&M	Atlanta
Milt Thompson	OF	Howard	Colorado
Marvin Freeman	P	Jackson St.	Chicago (AL)
Wes Chamberlain	OF	Jackson St.	Kansas City

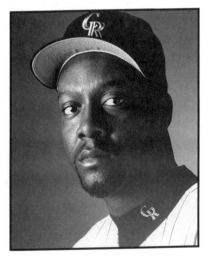 

(Both photos courtesy Colorado Rockies)

Marvin Freeman
Chicago (AL)
(Jackson State)

Trenidad Hubbard
San Francisco
(Southern University)

Name	Pos.	School	MLB Team
Dave Clark	OF	Jackson St.	Pittsburgh
Mike Farmer	P	Jackson St.	Colorado
Trenidad Hubbard	OF	Southern	San Francisco
Lenny Webster	OF	Grambling	Montreal

Black College
Sports From A-to-Z

A — A is for Avery Johnson of Southern University who plays point guard for the San Antonio Spurs.

B — B is for Bob Hayes of Florida A&M who was an Olympic champion in the 100-yard dash and a wide receiver with the Dallas Cowboys.

C — C is for Caldwell Jones of Albany State. He had three brothers, Charles, Wilbur and Major, who all attended the same college.

D — D is for Dr. Leroy Walker of Benedict College, who is the president of the United States Olympic Committee.

E — E is for Earl Monroe of Winston-Salem, who played for the Baltimore Bullets and the New York Knicks and is a member of the Basketball Hall of Fame.

F — F is for "Fang" as in Ron "Fang" Mitchell, head basketball coach of the Coppin State Eagles.

G — G is for Greg Lloyd of Fort Valley State, who plays linebacker for the Pittsburgh Steelers.

H — H is for Harry Carson of South Carolina State, who played linebacker for the New York Giants.

I — I is for Ivory Lee Brown of Arkansas Pine-Bluff, one of the leading rushers in black college football in 1990.

J — J is for Jake Gaither, head football coach of Florida A&M, who led the Rattlers to six black college football championships during his coaching career.

K — K is for Ken Houston of Prairie View A&M, who played strong safety for the Houston Oilers and the Washington Redskins.

L — L is for Larry Spriggs of Howard University, who played for the Los Angeles Lakers 1985 NBA championship team.

M — M is for Mildred McDaniel of Tuskeegee, who won a gold medal in the high jump in the 1956 Olympics.

N — N is for Nate Newton of Florida A&M, who plays guard for the Dallas Cowboys.

Ron "Fang" Mitchell, a four-time Mid-Eastern Athletic Conference coach of the year, has led the Coppin State College Eagles since 1986. (Photo courtesy of Coppin State College)

O — O is for Otis Taylor of Prairie View A&M, who was an All-Pro wide receiver with the Kansas City Chiefs.

P — P is for Paul "Tank" Younger of Grambling, who was Eddie Robinson's first player to make it to the NFL.

Q — Q is for Quinn, as in Paul Quinn College, which won the 1922 and 1924 SWAC championships in football.

R — R is for Rock Newman of Howard University, who manages heavyweight boxer Riddick Bowe.

S — S is for Sammie White of Grambling, who played wide receiver for the Minnesota Vikings

T — T is for Thomas "Hollywood" Henderson of Langston, who played linebacker for the Dallas Cowboys.

U — U is for Ulysses Curtis of Florida A&M, a Black College All-American football player in 1948.

V — V is for Vince Buck of Central State, who played defensive back for the New Orleans Saints for six years.

W — W is for Willie Lanier of Morgan State, who played linebacker for the Kansas City Chiefs.

X — X is for Xavier University which produced Don "Slick" Watts, who played professional basketball for the Seattle SuperSonics and the Houston Rockets.

Y — Y is for Yolanda Laney of Cheyney State, an All-American basketball player for the Lady Wolves.

Z — Z is for Zefross Moss of Alabama State, who plays tackle for the Detroit Lions.